Good M

MW00784083

Other Titles by Dick B.

Dr. Bob's Library: Books for Twelve Step Growth

Anne Smith's Journal, 1933-1939: A.A.'s Principles of Success

The Oxford Group & Alcoholics Anonymous

The Akron Genesis of Alcoholics Anonymous

New Light on Alcoholism: The A.A. Legacy from Sam Shoemaker

The Books Early AAs Read for Spiritual Growth

Courage to Change (with Bill Pittman)

The Good Book and The Big Book: A.A.'s Roots in the Bible

That Amazing Grace: The Role of Clarence and Grace S. in Alcoholics Anonymous

Turning Point: A Comprehensive History of Early A.A.'s Spiritual Roots and Successes

HOPE!: The Story of Geraldine D., Alina Lodge & Recovery

Utilizing Early A.A.'s Spiritual Roots for Recovery Today

Good Morning!

Quiet Time, Morning Watch, Meditation, and Early A.A.

Dick B.

Paradise Research Publications, Inc.
Kihei, Maui, Hawaii

Paradise Research Publications, Inc., PO Box 837, Kihei, HI 96753-0837

© 1996, 1998 by Anonymous. **All rights reserved**
Published 1996. Revised Edition 1998
Printed in the United States of America

This Paradise Research Publications Edition is published by arrangement with Good Book Publishing Company, PO Box 837, Kihei, HI 96753-0837

The publication of this volume does not imply affiliation with nor approval or endorsement from Alcoholics Anonymous World Services, Inc.

ISBN: 1-885803-22-2

Library of Congress Catalog Card Number: 96-68529

To Frank Costantino and The Bridge Builders of America

Thus saith the LORD, Let not the wise *man* glory in his wisdom, neither let the mighty *man* glory in his might, let not the rich *man* glory in his riches; But let him that glorieth glory in this, that he understandeth and knoweth me, that I *am* the LORD which exercise lovingkindness, judgment, and righteousness, in the earth: for in these *things* I delight, saith the LORD.

—Jeremiah 9:23,24

Contents

Preface to Revised Edition

This title fills the last, major, gap in my research and writing on the historical components of early A.A.'s spiritual roots.

I began with Dr. Bob's Library. Then to the vital importance of the spiritual journal Dr. Bob's wife, Anne Smith, assembled and shared with early AAs and their families at A.A.'s Akron birthplace. Then to the Oxford Group's contribution to early A.A.

Then to the writing and teaching of the Rev. Sam Shoemaker of New York's Calvary Episcopal Church. Then, to my bibliography of *all* the books early AAs read for spiritual growth. Then to *The Good Book* and its impact on A.A.'s own Big Book. For, as Dr. Bob said, it was to the Bible that AAs looked for their basic recovery ideas. There remained an historical segment virtually untouched by A.A. histories—yet considered an absolute "must" in the early days. That segment was *Quiet Time*—an Oxford Group name for the vital period Oxford Group people and the early AAs (who were an integral part of the Group) set aside for worship, prayer, meditation, and communion with God through Bible study, the use of devotionals, reading of literature, ordinary prayer, and listening to God. The practice occurred each morning, was (in a much altered form) translated into A.A.'s Big Book, and became the foundation for A.A.'s Eleventh Step suggestions. And it has almost vanished with today's helter-skelter use squibs in "reflection" and "meditation" books.

This, as now revised, deals with the origins, importance, and nature of quiet time and how it contributed to early A.A. ideas.

Acknowledgements

To my son Ken, believer, supporter, scholar, critic, and helper. Though they are applauded in other books, I'll again mention those whose contributions figured heavily in my research for this particular book—though their contributions occurred earlier.

Among the founding families: Sue Smith Windows and Betty and Bob Smith; John Seiberling, Dorothy Seiberling, and Mary Seiberling Huhn; Dorothy Williams Culver; Sally Shoemaker Robinson and Nickie Shoemaker Haggart.

Among Oxford Group people in America—Reverend Harry Almond, Mrs. Terence Blair, Richard Hadden, Mrs. W. Irving Harris, James Houck, T. Willard Hunter, James D. and Eleanor F. Newton, Richard Ruffin, L. Parks Shipley, Sr., and George Vondermuhll, Jr.; and abroad—Kenneth Belden, Sydney Cook, Michael Hutchinson, Garth Lean, and Dr. Robin Mowat.

A host of AAs and A.A. historians including: Mel B., Fr. Paul B., Dennis C., Ray G., Earl H., Gail L., Paul L., Frank M., Dale and Carol M., Bill P., John S., Dick S., George T., Danny and Denise W., Nell Wing, and Dr. Ernest Kurtz.

Special thanks to Paul Wood, Ph.D; Karen Plavan, Ph.D.; Jean LaCour, Ph.D; the Rev. Dr. Richard McCandless; Marcheta Scott; L. Parks Shipley, Sr.; Mrs. Walter Shipley; Leonard and Raymond (deceased); Martha Baker; Steve and Sue Foreman; Bob Koch (deceased); R. Brinkley Smithers (deceased); the Thomas Pike Foundation; Grace Snyder (deceased); and Mickey Evans.

1

What's It All About?

Prayer, meditation, and the use of meditation books in the Twelve Step and recovery programs of today do not remotely resemble the Quiet Time practices AAs used with such astonishing success in the earliest days. During A.A.'s formative period, the morning began with God. Prayer and meditation time, whether in the home or in meetings, was time spent in studying about God, learning about God, praying to God, and listening for His direction. It was a time which looked to the Bible *first*. If "devotionals" or "meditation" books were consulted, the reading of the books was subordinate to the purpose for which they were read: to learn more about the Bible, prayer, seeking God's guidance, and, of course, God Himself.

Peace, guidance, and the love of God were the much sought after objectives at the beginning of the day. Later in this book, we will see what has happened to those precious early practices. Prior to that, we will see the fullness of their origins in the Bible; and we will find out how A.A. root sources spent a very substantial amount of time at the beginning of each day in the whole Quiet Time process.

What this book is about, then, is where prayer and meditation with God really began, how it was practiced, how it can still be utilized with great success today, and how the present one page "squib" process can yet be returned to quality time with the

1

Creator—at the beginning, during, and end of the day. And we will start with A.A.'s great, and scarcely known, spiritual "teacher" and "co-founder," the Reverend Sam Shoemaker.

Dr. Samuel M. Shoemaker, Jr. (Rector of Calvary Episcopal Church in New York for twenty-five years) was credited by A.A. co-founder Bill Wilson as the "wellspring" of A.A.'s Twelve Step principles and attitudes.[1] Bill called Sam a "co-founder" of Alcoholics Anonymous.[2] And Bill could not have named a more abundant source for the inflow of spiritual ideas to early A.A. Yet, when AAs had their Twentieth Anniversary Convention in St. Louis in 1955, Sam Shoemaker was scarcely known or recognized as he approached the lectern. So stated Bill Wilson, the co-founder of Alcoholics Anonymous.[3]

Shoemaker wrote over thirty books, countless articles, and numerous pamphlets. He was named one of America's ten greatest preachers.[4] And on October 4, 1945, Shoemaker began a series of short radio talks on the American Broadcasting Company network. The talks carried the name "Gems For Thought." And the following extracts from Shoemaker's very first radio program illustrate the depth of the quiet time facet of early A.A.'s spiritual history and successes.

Good Morning!

Shoemaker said in his first broadcast:

> Good morning! I wonder how many times those words have been said today. There are about 130,000,000 of us in the United States alone. Probably each of us says them at least a dozen times. They are an expressed wish that each of us will have a

---

[1] Dick B., *New Light on Alcoholism: The A.A. Legacy from Sam Shoemaker* (Corte Madera, CA: Good Book Publishing Company, 1994), p. 3.

[2] Dick B., *New Light on Alcoholism*, p. 3.

[3] See *Alcoholics Anonymous Comes of Age* (New York: Alcoholics Anonymous World Services, Inc., 1957), p. 38.

[4] "Ten of the Greatest American Preachers." *Newsweek*. March 28, 1955.

good first half of the day, on the very good assumption that if the first half is good, the second half is likely to be. The morning sets the tone of the day. . . .

I'll tell you a secret; meet God first in the day, before you meet anybody else; and then you'll meet them in a different spirit.

May I tell you what we do in our house? When my wife and I get up, the first thing we reach for is our Bibles—not a cigarette, nor a drink, nor the morning paper—but our Bibles. We read a chapter or two. Then we get quiet and spend some time in prayer. Our older daughter usually comes in for this time of devotion with us. In quietness we pray for the people, the causes, the immediate responsibilities of the day, and ask God to direct us. . . . We ask Him for direction. We work out our plans together, we get clear if anything has gotten between us, we include our daughter in our plans and talk about any decisions she may have to make. The family prayer-time ought to be a kind of crucible in which human tensions are washed out and human problems solved by the advice and help of one another, as we all wait upon God. Bring the family and business problems before Him, ask Him about them, and trust Him to tell you. Begin the day that way, and I think you really will have a "good morning," and a good afternoon, and a good evening—and a good life.

A.A.'s Meditation Principles Were Borrowed

Bill Wilson said the following many times and in many ways.

A.A. was not invented![5]

[N]obody invented Alcoholics Anonymous.[6]

[5] *As Bill Sees It: The A.A. Way of Life . . . selected writings of A.A.'s co-founder* (New York: Alcoholics Anonymous World Services, Inc., 1967), p. 67.

[6] *The Language of the Heart: Bill W.'s Grapevine Writings* (New York: The AA Grapevine, Inc., 1988), p. 202.

As a society we must never become so vain as to suppose that
we have been the authors and inventors of a new religion. We
will humbly reflect that each of A.A.'s principles, *every one of
them*, has been borrowed from ancient sources (italics in
original).[7]

A.A.'s principles on prayer and meditation were, of course, no
exception. The language of A.A.'s Eleventh Step reads:

> Sought through prayer and meditation to improve our conscious
> contact with God *as we understood Him*, praying only for
> knowledge of His will for us and the power to carry that out.[8]

Even this language seems to have been borrowed from the
following statement by the popular Oxford Group writer Stephen
Foot: "I will ask God to show me His purpose for my life and
claim from Him the power to carry that purpose out."[9]

The instructions in A.A.'s basic textbook (for taking the Eleventh
Step) begin as follows:

> *Step Eleven* suggests prayer and meditation. We shouldn't be shy
> on this matter of prayer. Better men than we are using it
> constantly. It works, if we have the proper attitude and work at
> it. It would be easy to be vague about this matter. Yet, we
> believe we can make some definite and valuable suggestions.[10]

And whence came the material for A.A.'s Eleventh Step
instructions? In an article he wrote for A.A.'s official publication,

[7] *Alcoholics Anonymous Comes of Age: A Brief History of A.A.* (New York:
Alcoholics Anonymous World Services, Inc., 1957), p. 231.

[8] *Alcoholics Anonymous: The Story of How Many Thousands of Men and Women
Have Recovered from Alcoholism.* 3rd ed. (New York: Alcoholics Anonymous World
Services, Inc., 1976), p. 59.

[9] Foot, *Life Began Yesterday*, p. 11.

[10] *Alcoholics Anonymous*, pp. 85-86.

The Grapevine, Bill Wilson discussed the origins of A.A.'s First and Twelfth Steps. Then he said:

> Having now accounted for AA's Steps One and Twelve, it is natural that we should next ask, "Where did the early AAs find the material for the remaining ten Steps? Where did we learn about moral inventory, amends for harm done, turning our wills and lives over to God? Where did we learn about meditation and prayer and all the rest of it?" The spiritual substance of our remaining ten Steps came straight from Dr. Bob's and my own earlier association with the Oxford Groups, as they were then led in America by that Episcopal rector, Dr. Samuel Shoemaker.[11]

This discussion of borrowed ideas would not be complete without adding the following remarks by A.A.'s other co-founder Dr. Bob:

> It wasn't until 1938 that the teachings and efforts and studies that had been going on were crystallized in the form of the Twelve Steps. . . . We already had the basic ideas, though not in terse and tangible form. We got them, as I said, as a result of our study of the Good Book.[12]

Hence, when one has reviewed (as the author has done) the studies in the Bible by early AAs and also the principles of the Oxford Group of which AAs were then an integral part, he or she should have no difficulty finding the Biblical roots and the Oxford Group principles to which Bill and Dr. Bob referred.[13] In fact, the following quote illustrates part of the relationship between the basic A.A. ideas that were taken from the Bible and the principles

---

[11] *The Language of the Heart*, p. 298.

[12] *The Co-Founders of Alcoholics Anonymous: Biographical Sketches Their Last Major Talks* (New York: Alcoholics Anonymous World Services, Inc., 1972, 1975), p. 10.

[13] See Dick B., *The Good Book and The Big Book: A.A.'s Roots in the Bible* (San Rafael, CA: Paradise Research Publications, 1995), pp. 151-59; *Design for Living: The Oxford Group's Contribution to Early A.A.* (San Rafael, CA: Paradise Research Publications, 1995), pp. 227-36, 246-69, 319-22.

of the Oxford Group to which AAs belonged in their formative years:

> The principles of "The Oxford Group" are the principles of the Bible.[14]

The Frequent Quiet Time References in Early A.A.

We are not in the dark as to where early AAs obtained their prayer and meditation teachings. Only the roots and specifics are missing today.

Frank Amos, who was soon to become one of A.A.'s first nonalcoholic trustees, was dispatched to Akron, Ohio, in 1938 by John D. Rockefeller, Jr., to see what was going on in the fledgling society that was achieving such great success with alcoholics in Midwestern United States. Amos described part of the "Program" as follows:

> He [an alcoholic] must have devotions every morning—a "quiet time" of prayer and some reading from the Bible and other religious literature. Unless this is faithfully followed, there is grave danger of backsliding.[15]

Then A.A.'s official history and biography added these observations:

> The A.A. members of that time did not consider meetings necessary to maintain sobriety. They were simply "desirable." Morning devotion and "quiet time," however, were musts.[16]

---

[14] Sherwood Sunderland Day, *The Principles of The Group* (Great Britain: The Oxford Group, n.d.), p. 1.

[15] *DR. BOB and the Good Oldtimers, A biography with recollections of early A.A. in the Midwest* (New York: Alcoholics Anonymous World Services, Inc., 1980), p. 131.

[16] *DR. BOB*, p. 136.

Henrietta D. (the wife of A.A. Number Three) commented on the importance Dr. Bob's wife, Anne Ripley Smith, assigned to quiet time:

> She [Anne] would call me every single morning and ask me if I had had my quiet time. You were supposed to go by yourself with a pad and pencil and put down anything that came into your mind. Later in the day, it might come to you why. Probably for a year, she called me every single morning: "Did you have your quiet time? Did you get anything special out of it?" She was wonderful.[17]

In the spiritual journal she assembled in the 1930's, Dr. Bob's wife wrote extensively about prayer, meditation, and quiet time.[18] Anne shared from this journal with early AAs and their families as they came to the Smith home for meetings, teaching, and counsel.[19] And the following remarks by Anne in her journal illustrate the early A.A. view:

> *Daily Quiet Time.* This cannot be emphasized too much. Not a day should be missed. The early morning hours are best. It may be that more than one quiet time will be needed during the day. Whenever need arises one should stop and pray and listen. The method of holding quiet time varies some with each individual. All include prayer and Bible reading and study and patient listening to God.

Anne's daughter, Sue Smith Windows, typed a portion of her mother's journal and was present at many of the early morning meetings; and Sue reflected as follows on the morning quiet time in early A.A.:

---

[17] *DR. BOB*, p. 86.

[18] Dick B., *Anne Smith's Journal, 1933-1939: A.A.'s Principles of Success* (San Rafael, CA: Paradise Research Publications, 1994), pp. 53-64, 107-16.

[19] Dick B., *Anne Smith's Journal*, p. 9.

At that time [when "Dad and Mom and Bill were working out the program"] I was getting involved with the quiet times they had in the morning. The guys would come, and Mom would have her quiet time with them. There was a cookie salesman and he'd bring the stale cookies over, and we'd take up a collection for three pounds of coffee for 29 cents. Then they'd have their quiet time, which is a holdover from the Oxford Group, where they read the Bible, prayed and listened, and got guidance. Then they'd have coffee and cookies. This was early in the morning, when the sky was just starting to get light. Sometimes they'd get out of bed to do this.[20]

And A.A.'s Conference Approved literature showed the persistence of such quiet time practices, stating:

Morning quiet time continued to be an important part of the recovery program in 1938-1939, as did the spiritual reading from which the early members derived a good deal of their inspiration.[21]

The same A.A. biography pointed as follows to Dr. Bob's *own* continuance of the practice:

Prayer, of course, was an important part of Dr. Bob's faith. According to Paul S., "Dr. Bob's morning devotion consisted of a short prayer, a 20-minute study of a familiar verse from the Bible, and a quiet period of waiting for directions as to where he, that day, should find use for his talent. Having heard, he would religiously go about his Father's business, as he put it."[22]

A.A.'s other co-founder Bill Wilson and his wife Lois Wilson also continued a similar practice to the end of Bill's days, with Bill's

---

[20] Bob Smith and Sue Smith Windows, *Children of the Healer: The Story of Dr. Bob's Kids* (Park Ridge, IL: Parkside Publishing Corporation, 1992), pp. 43-44.

[21] *DR. BOB*, p. 150.

[22] *DR. BOB*, p. 314.

expressing the following regret over quiet time's disappearance from A.A.:

> I always felt that something was lost from A.A. when we stopped emphasizing the morning meditation. (Bill and Lois themselves, however, continued this practice together until his death, in 1971.)[23]

Many *other* early A.A. pioneers commented on the importance of the meditation practices.[24]

The Biblical and Oxford Group Roots

We will have much more to say about the roots of morning quiet time as our study progresses. But consider the following evidence pertaining to *morning* prayer and meditation.

The Good Book, as Dr. Bob and Bill described the Bible, said:

> Give ear to my words, O LORD, consider my meditation. Hearken unto the voice of my cry, my King and my God: for unto thee will I pray. My voice shalt thou hear in the morning, O LORD; in the morning will I direct *my prayer* unto thee, and will look up (Psalm 5:1-3).

> The Lord God hath given me the tongue of the learned, that I should know how to speak a word in season to *him that is* weary: he wakeneth morning by morning, he wakeneth mine ear to hear as the learned (Isaiah 50:4).

---

[23] *DR. BOB*, p. 178.

[24] Dick B., *The Akron Genesis of Alcoholics Anonymous* (Corte Madera, CA: Good Book Publishing Company, 1992), pp. 203-15; *That Amazing Grace: The Role of Clarence and Grace S. in Alcoholics Anonymous* (San Rafael, CA: Paradise Research Publications, 1996), pp. 26-38, 54, 56-58, 76, 88-92; *Alcoholics Anonymous*, 1st ed (New York City: Works Publishing Company, 1939), pp. 323, 347.

Several of the devotionals early AAs used attributed the origin of the "Morning Watch," or "Quiet Time," as it was called in the Oxford Group, to Psalm 5:3.[25] Authority for the Isaiah 50:4 root can be found in Oxford Group writings.[26]

As Dr. Bob's wife pointed out, there were individual variations in the meditation practices AAs borrowed from the Oxford Group. But most of the authoritative Oxford Group guides laid out the following elements, which we will detail at a later point:

1. Assigning a definite time first thing in the morning.[27]
2. Getting quiet, relaxed, and expectantly patient.[28]
3. Reading the Bible and devotionals before two-way prayer begins.[29]
4. Praying *to* God: confession, petition, thanksgiving, intercession.[30]
5. Listening for guidance *from* God.[31]
6. Writing down the thoughts received.[32]

[25] Dick B., *The Good Book and The Big Book*, p. 154. See also Nora Smith Holm, *The Runner's Bible* (New York: Houghton Mifflin Company, 1915), p. 158; *The Upper Room* for 5/9/35, 7/1/35, 7/22/37; Harry Emerson Fosdick, *The Meaning of Prayer* (New York: Association Press, 1915), p. 75.

[26] D. M. Prescott, *A New Day: Daily Readings for Our Time*, New ed. (London: Grosvenor Books, 1979), p. 1; Jack C. Winslow, *When I Awake: Thoughts on the Keeping of the Morning Watch* (London: Hodder & Stoughton, 1938), p. 13. Note that Winslow misquotes the chapter and verse in Isaiah.

[27] Samuel M. Shoemaker, Jr., *Realizing Religion* (New York: Association Press, 1923), pp. 65-66.

[28] Psalm 37:7; 46:10; Howard J. Rose, *The Quiet Time* (New York: The Oxford Group, n.d.), p. 3.

[29] 2 Timothy 2:15; Mary W. Tileston, *Daily Strength for Daily Needs* (Boston: Roberts Brothers, 1893), p. 68; *The Upper Room* for 4/27/38; S. M. Shoemaker, *How to Find God* (New York: Faith at Work, n.d.), p. 15.

[30] Matthew 26:41; Samuel M. Shoemaker, Jr., *The Conversion of the Church* (New York: Fleming H. Revell, 1932), p. 60.

[31] 1 Samuel 3:9; Garth Lean, *Cast Out Your Nets: Sharing Your Faith with Others* (London: Grosvenor, 1990), p. 25; Shoemaker, *The Conversion of the Church*, p. 60; Cecil Rose, *When Man Listens* (New York: Oxford University Press, 1937), pp. 30-35.

[32] Jeremiah 30:2; Hallen Viney, *How Do I Begin?* (New York: The Oxford Group, n.d.), p. 3.; Rose, *The Quiet Time*, p. 3.

7. Checking the messages to be sure of true guidance from God.[33]
8. Obedience to the guidance received.[34]

The thesis was and is that God spoke to the prophets of old; he spoke to men and women of God throughout the Bible; and He can and will speak to men and women today if they listen.[35] And there were several accepted Oxford Group guidebooks to the process, in addition to those written by Sam Shoemaker. Most were recommended by Shoemaker in his parish publication, *The Calvary Evangel*. And the very titles of these books and pamphlets disclose the underlying philosophy:

1. Eleanor Napier Forde, *The Guidance of God*.[36]
2. Burnett Hillman Streeter, *The God Who Speaks*.[37]
3. Cecil Rose, *When Man Listens*.[38]
4. Howard J. Rose, *The Quiet Time*.[39]
5. Hallen Viney, *How do I Begin?*[40]

Oxford Group Founder Dr. Frank N. D. Buchman became famous for an oft-repeated statement he delivered in Great Britain on July 26, 1936:

When man listens, God speaks. When man obeys, God acts.[41]

---

[33] Howard Rose, *The Quiet Time*, p. 2; A. J. Russell, *For Sinners Only* (London: Hodder & Stoughton, 1932), p. 94.

[34] John 7:17; Dick B., *The Oxford Group & Alcoholics Anonymous* (Kihei, HI: Paradise Research Publications, Inc., 1998), pp. 272-75.

[35] Dick B., *The Oxford Group & Alcoholics Anonymous*, pp. 227-36.

[36] Eleanor Napier Forde, *The Guidance of God* (London: The Oxford Group, 1930).

[37] Burnett Hillman Streeter, *The God Who Speaks*, 1st ed. (London: Macmillan & Co., Ltd., 1936).

[38] Cecil Rose, *When Man Listens* (New York: Oxford University Press, 1937).

[39] Howard J. Rose, *The Quiet Time* (New York: The Oxford Group, n.d.).

[40] Hallen Viney, *How Do I Begin?* (New York: The Oxford Group, n.d.).

[41] Frank N. D. Buchman, *Remaking the World: The Speeches of Frank N. D. Buchman* (London: Blandford Press, 1961), pp. 35, 42.

Described by one of his biographers as "soaked in the Bible," Frank Buchman quoted Scripture to back up this idea about the will of God and the importance of man's listening for the voice of God to determine God's particular will for him:

> Obey my voice, and I will be your God, and ye shall be my people: and walk ye in all the ways that I have commanded you, that it may be well unto you (Jeremiah 7:23).[42]

Bill Wilson's wife, Lois, who could hardly be counted as an Oxford Group enthusiast, nonetheless penned in her "Oxford Group Notes" the following:

---

[42] Buchman, *Remaking the World*, p. 8. For some Roman Catholic ideas and expressions of difficulty with these concepts, see Jules J. Toner, S.J., *Discerning God's Will: Ignatius of Loyola's Teaching on Christian Decision Making* (St. Louis, MO: Institute of Jesuit Sources, 1991); Joseph F. Eagan, S.J., S.T.D., *Restoration And Renewal: The Church in the Third Millennium* (Kansas City, MO: Sheed & Ward, 1995), pp. 34-36; James J. Megivern, *Official Catholic Teachings: Bible Interpretation* ["Dei Verbum, Dogmatic Constitution on Divine Revelation," November 18, 1965] (Wilmington, NC: A Consortium Book from McGrath Publishing Company, 1978), pp. 403-17; John C. Ford, S.J., *Moral Re-Armament and Alcoholics Anonymous* (N.C.C.A. "Blue Book", Vol. 10., 1960): "MRA is a religious movement with a fundamentally Protestant, theological orientation, and involves Catholics in serious dangers to their faith"; Robert Fitzgerald, S.J., *The Soul of Sponsorship: The Friendship of Fr. Ed Dowling, S.J. and Bill Wilson in Letters* (Center City, MN: Hazelden, 1995), pp. 55-63, 75-82; Rev. Clair M. Dinger, S.T.L., *Moral Re-Armament: A Study of Its Technical and Religious Nature in the Light of Catholic Teaching* (Washington, D.C.: The Catholic University of America Press, 1961), pp. 41-60. See particularly: "How different MRA teaching on divine guidance is from the tenets of Catholic theology can be readily seen from the following brief examination of Catholic doctrine on the subject" (p.46). And, at the conclusion: "Divine guidance" itself is ultimately the only authentication for "divine guidance." And the adherents of MRA blindly dance around the edge of this vicious circle, not realizing the grave dangers involved! The Catholic, on the other hand, has '. . . precise and subtle rules for judging them [inspirations]" which the Church, the infallible guide in the religious life, has laid down. Where such infallibility is lacking there is the grave temptation to fill up this void with substitutes" (pp. 59-60).

A supernatural network over live wires. Why not the voice of God in every parliament, every business? Every last man in every last place. Definite adequate, accurate information from God.[43]

What We Will Do

What is it all about, then?

The Bible is replete with references to the fact that holy men of God with the spirit of God *upon* them, and born again believers with the spirit of God *in* them, could and did receive revelation from God.[44] And can today!

In their own way, the Oxford Group people seized upon these and other Biblical references and evolved practices by which they believed any person (who had surrendered his life to God) could hear from God and profit from the divinely revealed message. The proviso was that he or she be willing to ask for God's guidance, study God's Word, pray, listen, check, and obey the leading thoughts indicative of God's particular will for that person.

As we pointed out in the earlier footnote, this has raised some Roman Catholic hackles more than a few times in A.A.'s history and in the history of the Oxford Group before it. As Father Robert Fitzgerald put it concerning Bill's interest in the Roman Catholic Church, "The doctrine of papal infallibility stopped him. . . . [and Bill wrote Father Ed Dowling:] It is ever so hard to believe that any human beings, now matter who, are able to be infallible about anything. There seems to be so little evidence all through the centuries that God intends to work that way."[45]

---

[43] See Dick B., *New Light on Alcoholism*, p. 337, quoting from page 3 of Lois Wilson's Oxford Group Notes which the author inspected and copied at the archives in the Wilson home at Stepping Stones, in Bedford Hills, New York. Compare the language used by Frank Buchman and cited on page 337, in footnote 1, of *New Light on Alcoholism*.

[44] See Numbers 11:25; Isaiah 11:2; Matthew 12:18; Acts 9:3-20; 10:1-19; 1 Corinthians 12:7-11; Galatians 1:11-12; 2 Timothy 3:16; 2 Peter 1:20-21.

[45] Fitzgerald, *The Soul of Sponsorship*, pp. 47, 49.

We will be exploring how it all began in the Bible. We will
examine the Quiet Time practices themselves. We will see how
"meditation," as it was described in the Bible, progressed through
history. We will look at the "helpful books" the "alcoholic squad
of the Oxford Group" in Akron and other Oxford Group
fellowships of that day used to guide them and teach them in their
devotions. We will try to learn what early AAs themselves actually
borrowed from this historical framework. And we will determine
how the history of the quiet time, morning watch, and meditation
can be used today to put Twelve Step people and others in touch
with the same will of God, "voice" of God, power of God, love
of God, and deliverance by God that enabled early AAs to claim
such an astonishing success rate.[46]

---

[46] For a discussion and documentation of the success rate claimed by early AAs, and
a comparison with the probable success rate in today's A.A., see Dick B., *The Good
Book and The Big Book*, pp. 7-10; *Design for Living*, pp. 3-8.

2

It Began in the Bible

The Will of God

Sam Shoemaker taught that God's *general will* is to be found in the Scriptures.[1] Later, he wrote: "The Bible from one end to the other tells us about Him [God], about His will for man and the world."[2] Phrasing the "general will" idea slightly differently, the Oxford Group's progenitors said the Bible contains God's *universal will.*[3] Professor Henry Drummond (who was widely quoted by Shoemaker and whose books were read by A.A.'s co-founder Dr. Bob) wrote: "The Bible is God's will in words, in formal thoughts, in grace."[4] Drummond gave the Ten Commandments and the Beatitudes of Christ as examples.[5] AAs themselves frequently spoke of the necessity for knowing the will of God; and

---

[1] Samuel M. Shoemaker, Jr., *The Conversion of the Church* (New York: Fleming H. Revell, 1932), pp. 49-50; *A Young Man's View of the Ministry* (New York: Association Press, 1923), p. 78.

[2] Samuel M. Shoemaker, *Christ and This Crisis* (New York: Fleming H. Revell, 1943), p. 106.

[3] Henry Drummond, *The Ideal Life: Addresses Hitherto Unpublished* (New York: Hodder & Stoughton, 1897), pp. 268-71; Henry B. Wright, *The Will of God and a Man's Lifework* (New York: The Young Men's Christian Association Press, 1909), p. 137.

[4] Drummond, *The Ideal Life*, p. 268.

[5] Drummond, *The Ideal Life*, pp. 270-71; see also, Wright, *The Will of God*, p. 137.

since their spiritual sources all taught that God's universal will is to be found in the Bible, we think it vital to start with the Bible to find what Scripture has to say about getting in touch with, and knowing God, and His will, in the morning and throughout the day, by prayer, meditation, and the study of His word.[6]

The Morning Watch

Before the captivity, the Hebrews divided the night into three "watches": (1) From sunset to ten p.m., (2) from ten p.m. to two a.m., and (3) from two a.m. to sunrise. The first watch period was called the "beginning of the watches;"[7] the second, the "middle watch;"[8] and the third, the "morning watch."[9] Collectively, the three were called the "night watches."[10]

When the Israelites became subject to Roman power, most adopted the Roman method of dividing the watches—increasing the number from three to four: (1) Evening watch—sunset to 9:00 p.m.;[11] (2) Midnight watch—9:00 p.m. to midnight;[12] (3) Cock-crowing watch—midnight to 3:00 a.m.;[13] and (4) Morning watch 3:00 a.m. to sunrise.[14]

The watches marked the time in only a general way. The "watch," as a word, had special significance in Bible times

---

[6] For the many examples of A.A. concern over the will of God (particularly as expressed in the language of its Eleventh Step), see *Alcoholics Anonymous*, 3rd ed. (New York: Alcoholics Anonymous World Services, Inc., 1976), pp. 59, 63, 67, 85, 87; *Alcoholics Anonymous Comes of Age* (New York: Alcoholics Anonymous World Services, 1979), p. 105; Dick B., *The Good Book and The Big Book: A.A.'s Roots in the Bible* (San Rafael, CA: Paradise Research Publications, 1995), p. 69.

[7] Lamentations 2:19.

[8] Judges 7:19.

[9] Exodus 14:24; 1 Samuel 11:11.

[10] Psalms 63:6; 119:148.

[11] Mark 13:35.

[12] Luke 12:38.

[13] Luke 12:38.

[14] Matthew 14:25; Mark 6:48.

primarily because of its relationship to the function of the "watchmen." The cities of old relied upon the watchmen for protection. Men were employed to watch day and night on the top of the city walls and especially by the gates.[15] Other watchmen had the duty of patrolling the streets of the city and preserving order.[16] The specific times given above must therefore be understood only in terms of approximations. We will examine primarily the "morning watch," which ended at sunrise. The Hebrew and Greek texts' references to "watch" speak of a "watch," a "guard," a "time during which guard was kept," a "guarding," and a "time of watch."[17]

In His Word, God ascribed special significance to the watches, as far as prayer and meditation were concerned. And the morning—sunrise—the end of the morning watch—was often mentioned in this connection:

> Thus will I bless thee while I live: I will lift up my hands in thy name. My soul shall be satisfied as *with* marrow and fatness; and my mouth shall praise *thee* with joyful lips. When I remember thee upon my bed, *and* meditate on thee in the *night* watches (Psalm 63:4-6).

> Arise, cry out in the night: in the beginning of the watches pour out thine heart like water before the face of the Lord . . . (Lamentations 2:19).

> Give ear to my words, O Lord, consider my meditation. Hearken unto the voice of my cry, my King, and My God: for unto thee will I pray. My voice shalt thou hear in the morning, O Lord; in

---

[15] E.g., 2 Samuel 18:26; James M. Freeman, *Manners and Customs of the Bible* (Plainfield, New Jersey: Logos International, 1972), p. 147.

[16] E.g., Song of Solomon 3:3; Freeman, *Manners and Customs of the Bible*, p. 248.

[17] For discussions of the watches, see *New Bible Dictionary*, 2d ed. (Wheaton, IL: Tyndale House, 1982), pp. 1242-43; *Vine's Expository Dictionary of Old and New Testament Words* (New York: Fleming H. Revell, 1981), p. 200; *The Abingdon Bible Commentary* (New York: Abingdon Press, 1920), p. 77a; *Wilson's Old Testament Word Studies* (McLean, VA: Mac Donald Publishing Co., n.d.), p. 474.

the morning will I direct *my prayer* unto thee, and will look up (Psalm 5:3-5).

But I will sing of thy power; yea I will sing aloud of thy mercy in the morning: for thou hast been my defence and refuge in the day of my trouble (Psalm 59:16).

But unto thee have I cried, O Lord; and in the morning shall my prayer prevent [precede] thee (Psalm 88:13).

It is a good *thing* to give thanks unto the Lord, and to sing praises unto thy name, O most High: To shew forth thy loving-kindness in the morning, and thy faithfulness every night (Psalm 92:1-2).

Cause me to hear thy loving-kindness in the morning; for in thee do I trust: cause me to know the way wherein I should walk; for I lift up my soul unto thee. Deliver me, O Lord, from mine enemies: I flee unto thee to hide me. Teach me to do thy will; for thou *art* my God: thy spirit *is* good; lead me into the land of uprightness. Quicken me, O Lord, for thy name's sake: for thy righteousness' sake bring my soul out of trouble (Psalm 143:8-11).[18]

The Lord God hath given me the tongue of the learned, that I should know how to speak a word in season to *him that is* weary: he wakeneth morning by morning, he wakeneth mine ear to hear as the learned. The Lord God hath opened mine ear, and I was not rebellious, neither turned away back (Isaiah 50:4-5).

The Bible As the Word of God

In the Old Testament, "the word (*dabar*) of God" is used 394 times of a divine communication which comes from God to men in the form of commandment, prophecy, warning or

---

[18] See K. D. Belden, *Meeting Moral Re-Armament* (London: Grosvenor Books, 1979), p. 26; *The Hour of the Helicopter* (Somerset, England: Linden Hall, 1992), p. 21.

encouragement.[19] From beginning to end, the Bible speaks of communications from God as the "word of God" or the "word of the Lord." The words of God collectively are spoken of as God's "Word." A.A. sources spoke often and authoritatively of the Bible as *the* Word of God.[20] And these sources were agreed that one who wished to learn the "will of God" should start with the "word of God."[21]

The following verses from the Old Testament illustrate the language in the Bible itself which characterized the Bible and its words as the Word of God:

After these things the word of the Lord came unto Abram in a vision, saying, Fear not, Abram: I *am* thy shield, *and* thy exceeding great reward (Genesis 15:1).

And the child Samuel ministered unto the Lord before Eli. And the word of the Lord was precious in those days; *there was* no open vision (1 Samuel 3:1).

Thy word have I hid in mine heart, that I might not sin against thee (Psalm 119:11).

---

[19] *New Bible Dictionary*, p. 1259.

[20] See, for example, F. B. Meyer, *The Secret of Guidance* (New York: Fleming H. Revell, 1896), p. 120; Henry Drummond, *The Ideal Life*, pp. 227-320; William R. Moody, *The Life of D. L. Moody* (New York: Fleming H. Revell, 1920), pp. 497, 19; Wright, *The Will of God and a Man's Lifework*, p. 137; Donald W. Carruthers, *How to Find Reality in Your Morning Devotions* (Pennsylvania: State College, n.d.), p. 1; Jack C. Winslow, *When I Awake* (London: Hodder & Stoughton, 1938), p. 62; "Vital Touch with God" (Reprint from *The Evangel*, n.d.), p. 5. For a discussion of the primary A.A. sources, see Dick B., *Design for Living: The Oxford Group Contribution to Early A.A.* (San Rafael, CA: Paradise Research Publications, 1995), pp. 1-67; *The Good Book and The Big Book*, pp. 12-38.

[21] See, for example, Samuel M. Shoemaker's usages in *Realizing Religion* (New York: Association Press, 1933), pp. 58-62; *A Young Man's View of the Ministry*, p. 78; *Twice-Born Ministers* (New York: Fleming H. Revell, 1929), pp. 184-185; *The Conversion of the Church*, pp. 49-50; *Christ and This Crisis*, p. 106.

Thy word *is* true *from* the beginning: and every one of thy righteous judgments *endureth* forever (Psalm 119:160).

I rejoice at thy word, as one that findeth great spoil (Psalm 119:162).

The word of the Lord came expressly unto Ezekiel (Ezekiel 1:3).[22]

And say unto the Ammonites, Hear the word of the Lord God; Thus saith the Lord God . . . (Ezekiel 25:3).

The burden of the word of the Lord to Israel by Malachi (Malachi 1:1).

In the Gospels, Jesus Christ characterized God's Word as follows:

I have given them thy word; and the world hath hated them, because they are not of the world, even as I am not of the world (John 17:14).

Sanctify them through thy truth: thy word is truth (John 17:17).

Now the parable is this: The seed is the word of God (Luke 8:11).

In 1 Thessalonians 2:13, the Apostle Paul said the following about the word of God:

For this cause also thank we God without ceasing, because when ye received the word of God which ye heard of us, ye received it not *as* the word of men, but as it is in truth, the word of God, which effectually worketh also in you that believe.

---

[22] See discussion in Winslow, *When I Awake*, p. 49.

In Hebrews 4:12, Paul said:

> For the word of God *is* quick and powerful, and sharper than
> any twoedged sword, piercing even to the dividing asunder of
> soul and spirit, and of the joints and marrow, and *is* a discerner
> of the thoughts and intents of the heart.

And Revelation, the final book of the Bible, states in Chapter 1,
verses 1-3:

> The Revelation of Jesus Christ, which God gave unto him, to
> shew unto his servants things which must shortly come to pass;
> and he sent and signified it by his angel unto his servant John:
>
> Who bare record of the word of God, and of the testimony of
> Jesus Christ, and of all things that he saw.
>
> Blessed is he that readeth, and they that hear the words of this
> prophecy, and keep those things which are written therein: for
> the time is at hand.

The Bible's Explanation of How
God Revealed His Written Word

The Old Testament frequently indicated how the word of God was
revealed to people, namely by vision (Isaiah 1:1-2; Habakkuk 2:2-
3),[23] by word (Jeremiah 1:2-4), and by instruction of the spirit
(Nehemiah 9:20; Psalm 143:10; Proverbs 1:3; Ezekiel 2:2).[24]
The New Testament further explained that this word of God was

---

[23] See Winslow, *When I Awake*, p. 49.

[24] See Nora Smith Holm, *The Runner's Bible* (New York: Houghton Mifflin, 1915),
p. 52.

revealed to the spirit of believers by God, who *is* spirit.[25] The following verses elaborated:

> Knowing this first, that no prophecy of the scripture is of any private interpretation. For the prophecy came not in old time by the will of man: but holy men of God spake *as they were* moved by the Holy Ghost (2 Peter 1:20-21).[26]

> All scripture *is* given by inspiration of God, and *is* profitable for doctrine, for reproof, for correction, for instruction in righteousness (2 Timothy 3:16).[27]

> But I certify you, brethren, that the gospel which was preached of me is not after man. For I neither received it of man, neither was I taught it, but by the revelation of Jesus Christ (Galatians 1:11-12).[28]

---

[25] John 4:24: "God *is* a Spirit." The word "a" should be deleted as it is not used in Greek texts. The correct translation would be "God *is* [added by King James Version] Spirit." See also as to the Comforter or Holy Spirit or Spirit of truth which will teach: John 14:16, 26; 15:26; 16:7-15; Acts 1:4, 5, 8; and Holm, *The Runner's Bible*, pp. 16, 17, 104; Harry Almond, *Foundations for Faith*, 2d ed. (London: Grosvenor, 1980), p. 23.

[26] See Holm, *The Runner's Bible*, p. 18; Wright, *The Will of God*, p. 147.

[27] See E. Stanley Jones, *Victorious Living* (New York: Abingdon Press, 1936), p. 262. As to Dwight L. Moody, the evangelist, see Dick B., *Design for Living*, p. 44. For the Roman Catholic view of the Scripture, see the Encyclical Letter of Pope Pius XII, "Divino Afflante Spiritu," September 30, 1943, in James J. Megivern, *Official Catholic Teachings: Bible Interpretation* (Wilmington, NC: McGrath Publishing Company, 1978), p. 316.

[28] See Wright, *The Will of God*, p. 145; Burnett Hillman Streeter, *The God Who Speaks* (London: MacMillan and Co., 1936), p. 91; Ebenezer Macmillan, *Seeking and Finding* (New York: Harper & Brothers, 1933), p. 140.

The Biblical Commandments on
Meditation, Study, and Prayer

Meditate in the Word of God!

A word about "meditation." Merriam Webster's Collegiate Dictionary, Tenth Edition, defines "meditate" in terms of engaging in contemplation or reflection and, when directed at an object, "to focus one's thoughts on: reflect on or ponder over." Thus when the Bible speaks of "meditating," as it often does, it is speaking of focusing thoughts on, pondering over, and studying *the word of God*.[29] That interpretation is usually clear from the verse itself and certainly from the context.

The following are some of the many verses which speak of "meditating" on God, His work, and His word. Some of the verses were mentioned in the religious literature early AAs read for spiritual growth.[30] The word of God is variously referred to as His word, His commandments, His precepts, His teachings, His statutes, and His law:

My meditation of him [God] shall be sweet: I will be glad in the Lord (Psalm 104:34).[31]

I will meditate also of all thy work, and talk of thy doings. Thy way, O God, *is* in the sanctuary: who *is* so great a God as *our* God. Thou *art* the God that doest wonders: thou has declared thy strength among the people (Psalm 77:12-14).

But his delight is in the law of the Lord; and in his law doth he meditate day and night. And he shall be like a tree planted by the

---

[29] See Spiros Zodhiates, *The Hebrew-Greek Key Study Bible*, rev. ed. (AMG Publishers, 1991); see page 32 of the Hebrew and Chaldee Dictionary portion, number 1897.

[30] For a list of these materials, see Dick B., *The Books Early AAs Read for Spiritual Growth*, 6th ed. (Kihei, HI: Paradise Research Publications, Inc., 1998).

[31] See Holm, *The Runner's Bible*, p. 38.

rivers of water, that bringeth forth his fruit in his season; his leaf also shall not wither; and whatsoever he doeth shall prosper (Psalm 1:2-3).[32]

O how love I thy law! it *is* my meditation all day (Psalm 119:97).

I have more understanding than all my teachers: for thy testimonies *are* my meditation (Psalm 119:99).

I will meditate in thy precepts, and have respect unto thy ways. I will delight myself in thy statutes: I will not forget thy word (Psalms 119:15-16).

Let the proud be ashamed; for they dealt perversely with me without a cause: but I will meditate in thy precepts (Psalm 119:78).

My hands also will lift up unto thy commandments, which I have loved; and I will meditate in thy statutes (Psalm 119:48).

Mine eyes prevent [preccdc] the *night* watches, that I might meditate in thy word (Psalm 119:148).

When the Old Testament spoke of meditation, it described a thinking process which focused thoughts on, pondered, and studied about God, His works, and His word. And in addressing his faithful helper Timothy, Paul warned against seducing spirits and doctrines of devils with lies in hypocrisy. He urged the word of God and prayer and the rejection of profane and old wives fables. He urged reading, exhortation, and doctrine. He concluded:

Meditate upon these things; give thyself wholly to them; that thy profiting may appear to all. Take heed unto thyself, and unto the

---

[32] Mary Wilder Tileston, *Daily Strength for Daily Needs* (New York: Grosset & Dunlap, 1884), p. 258.

doctrine; continue in them; for in doing this thou shalt both save thyself, and them that hear thee (1 Timothy 4:15-16).

Study the Scriptures!

What did the Word of God have to say about the meditation *process*?

Jesus Christ made three suggestions to his hearers. The suggestions were to enable doubters to learn whether Jesus was actually speaking for God. He suggested to his listeners: (1) Search the Scriptures because they actually testify of me (Jesus Christ). (2) If you are wondering whether my teachings are simply my own idea or whether they represent the word and will of God, you should act on those teachings. Then, said Jesus, you will learn for yourself from your experience whose will they represent. (3) You would not ask some of the questions you ask if you knew the scriptures and the power of God.

In the following verses, Jesus made those points clear:

Search the scriptures; for in them ye think ye have eternal life: and they are they which testify of me (John 5:39).[33]

Jesus answered them, and said, My doctrine is not mine, but his that sent me. If any man will do his will, he shall know of the doctrine, *whether* it be of God, or whether I speak of myself (John 7:16-17).[34]

Jesus answered and said unto them, Ye do err, not knowing the scriptures, nor the power of God (Matthew 22:29).[35]

---

[33] See Holm, *The Runner's Bible*, p. 51; *The Upper Room* for 8/12/38; Dick B., *New Light on Alcoholism* (Corte Madera, CA: Good Book Publishing Company, 1994), p. 270.

[34] See Meyer, *The Secret of Guidance*, p. 11; Wright, *The Will of God*, pp. 19, 117 *et. seq.*; Glenn Clark, *I Will Lift Up Mine Eyes* (New York: Harper & Row, 1937), p. 27; *The Upper Room* for 4/26/35; Dick B., *New Light on Alcoholism*, pp. 43, 101, 110, 117, 118, 121, 148, 181, 208, 227, 230, 267, 294, 298, 316.

[35] See Jones, *Victorious Living*, p. 262; Holm, *The Runner's Bible*, p. 51.

Believers in the first century Christian Church heeded what they were taught about the word of God. However, they also checked out the teachings against the word itself to be sure the teachings conformed to the word of God. Speaking of those from Berea, the Book of Acts said:

These [the believers from Berea] were more noble than those in Thessalonica, in that they received the word with all readiness of mind, and searched the scriptures daily, whether those things were so. Therefore many of them believed; also of honourable women which were Greeks, and of men, not a few (Acts: 17:11-12).

Finally, Paul wrote Timothy that the word of God was to be studied and "worked" carefully to assure that it was being correctly interpreted:

Study to shew thyself approved unto God, a workman that needeth not to be ashamed, rightly dividing the word of truth. But shun profane *and* vain babblings: for they will increase unto more ungodliness (2 Timothy 2:15-16).[36]

---

[36] See Tileston, *Daily Strength for Daily Needs*, p. 68; Jones, *Victorious Living*, p. 327; *The Upper Room* for 4/27/38, 9/20/38; Oswald Chambers, *My Utmost for His Highest* (New Jersey: Barbour & Company, 1963), p. 350. As can be seen from these citations, this idea was certainly not confined to the Oxford Group; but, for quite some time, Roman Catholics often laid their criticism of "guidance" and other Protestant ideas in early A.A. at the feet of Frank Buchman's movement. See Dinger, *supra*, pp. 125-30: [Cardinal Hinsley in 1938:] "no Catholic can join it to take any active part in it. . . ;" [the Hierarchy in 1946:] "Catholics should be warned not to attend their meetings or gatherings, even as spectators;" [Cardinal Frings in 1950:] ". . . dangerous religious syncretism. . .;" [the Holy Office to the Bishops throughout the world in 1951:] ". . . it is not fitting that the faithful should accept posts of responsibility in Moral Re-Armament, and especially not fitting that they should join the so-called 'policy team';" [Cardinal Schuster in 1952:] "This movement, Protestant in origin and structure . . . is dangerous. . .;" [Monsignor Brown, Bishop of Galway:] ". . . the Oxford Group forms a heretical sect. . . . [N]o Catholic can become a member without rejecting the teaching of the Church." For the fears such positions caused Bill Wilson, see *Pass It On* (New York: Alcoholics Anonymous World Services, Inc., 1984), p. 171; *DR. BOB and the*
(continued...)

The Book of James, a favorite in early A.A., stated:

> Wherefore lay apart all filthiness and superfluity of naughtiness, and receive with meekness the engrafted word, which is able to save your souls. But be ye doers of the word, and not hearers only, deceiving your own selves (James 1:21-22).[37]

Meditate and Pray in the Morning!

The most recognized source in God's word pertaining to *morning* prayer and meditation can be found in Psalm 5:1-3:

> Give ear to my words, O Lord, consider my meditation. Hearken unto the voice of my cry, my King, and my God: for unto thee will I pray. My voice shalt thou hear in the morning, O Lord; in the morning will I direct *my prayer* unto thee, and will look up.

The foregoing verses were cited in several of the spiritual books and pamphlets giving rise to early A.A. ideas concerning morning prayers, devotions, and meditation.[38] And the following verses advocated starting afresh with God each morning:

> But unto thee have I cried, O Lord; and in the morning shall my prayer prevent [precede] thee (Psalm 88:13).[39]

---

[36] (...continued)
Good Oldtimers (New York: Alcoholics Anonymous World Services, Inc., 1980), pp. 155-70. For a later and much different view, see *TRUE DIALOGUE: Two addresses at Harvard University by His Eminence Franz Cardinal Koenig, former Archbishop of Vienna* (Newberg, Oregon: The Barclay Press, 1986) and Eagan, *supra*, pp. 33-36, 39, 123.

[37] See Holm, *The Runner's Bible*, p. 47; Roger Hicks, *How to Read the Bible* (Moral Re-Armament, n.d.), p. 33.

[38] *The Upper Room* for 5/9/35, May 9; Holm, *The Runner's Bible*, p. 158 and dedication page; E. Stanley Jones, *Victorious Living*, p. 68; Harry Emerson Fosdick, *The Meaning of Prayer* (New York: Association Press, 1915), p. 75; Clarence I. Benson, *The Eight Points of the Oxford Group* (London: Humphrey Milford, Oxford University Press, 1936), p. 79.

[39] Winslow, *When I Awake*, p. 17; Fosdick, *The Meaning of Prayer*, p. 74.

And in the morning, then ye shall see the glory of the Lord (Exodus 16:7).[40]

Cause me to hear thy lovingkindness in the morning; for in thee do I trust; cause me to know the way wherein I should walk; for I lift up my soul unto thee (Psalm 143:8).[41]

It is a good thing to give thanks unto the Lord, and to sing praises unto thy name, O most High; To shew forth thy lovingkindness in the morning, and thy faithfulness every night (Psalm 92:1-2).

Lamentations 2:19 suggested going to God in the earliest night watches:

Arise, cry out in the night: in the beginning of the watches pour out thine heart like water before the face of the Lord: lift up thy hands toward him for the life of thy young children, that faint for hunger in the top of every street.

Relax, Be Patient, Be Still, Listen, Await Direction!

The stance of the believer was to be one of rest, patience, stillness, waiting upon God in silence, expecting God to do the directing:

Rest in the Lord, and wait patiently for him: fret not thyself because of him who prospereth in his way, because of the man who bringeth wicked devices to pass (Psalm 37:7).[42]

---

[40] See Tileston, *Daily Strength for Daily Needs*, p. 183.

[41] Holm, *The Runner's Bible*, p. 158; Streeter, *The God Who Speaks*, p. 115; K. D. Belden, *The Hour of the Helicopter* (Somerset, England: Linden Hall, 1992), p. 21; *Meeting Moral Re-Armament* (London: Grosvenor Books, 1979), p. 26.

[42] See Tileston, *Daily Strength for Daily Needs*, p. 140; Holm, *The Runner's Bible*, p. 95; Howard J. Rose, *The Quiet Time* (The Oxford Group, n.d.), p. 3.

Be still, and know that I *am* God: I will be exalted among the heathen, I will be exalted in the earth (Psalm 46:10).[43]

Trust in the Lord with all thine heart; and lean not unto thine own understanding. In all thy ways acknowledge him, and he shall direct thy paths (Proverbs 3:5-6).[44]

Let the words of my mouth and the meditation of my heart, be acceptable in thy sight, O Lord, my strength, and my redeemer (Psalm 19:14).

Order my steps in thy word: and let not any iniquity have dominion over me (Psalm 119:133).

My soul *waiteth* for the Lord more than they that watch for the morning: I *say, more than* they that watch for the morning (Psalm 130:6).

My soul, wait thou only upon God: for my expectation is from him. He *is* my rock and my salvation: *he is* my defence; I shall not be moved. In God *is* my salvation and my glory: the rock of my strength, *and* my refuge, *is* in God. Trust in him at all times: ye people, pour out your heart before him: God is a refuge for us. Selah (Psalm 62:5-8).[45]

---

[43] See Rose, *The Quiet Time*, pp. 1,2; *The Upper Room* for 6/23/35; Benson, *The Eight Points of the Oxford Group*, p. 63; Chambers, *My Utmost for His Highest*, p. 41.

[44] Meyer, *The Secret of Guidance*, p. 7; Rose, *The Quiet Time*, p. 2; Holm, *The Runner's Bible*, p. 126; *The Upper Room*, for 5/15/35; Tileston, *Daily Strength for Daily Needs*, p. 31; Glenn Clark, *I Will Lift Up Mine Eyes* (New York: Harper & Row, 1937), pp. 18, 28, 88, 151; Streeter, *The God Who Speaks*, p. 191; Dick B., *Dr. Bob's Library: Books for Twelve Step Growth* (San Rafael, CA: Paradise Research Publications, 1994), pp. 96-97.

[45] See Fosdick, *The Meaning of Prayer*, p. 46.

Speak, Lord; for thy servant heareth (1 Samuel 3:9).[46]

Lord, what wilt thou have me to do? (Acts 9:6).[47]

Search me, O God, and know my heart: try me, and know my thoughts (Psalm 139:23).[48]

Watch, Continue in Prayer, Give Thanks, Don't Be Anxious!

Watch and pray (Matthew 26:41; Mark 13:33; Luke 21:36).[49]

Offer unto God thanksgiving; and pay thy vows unto the Most High. And call upon me in the day of trouble; I will deliver thee, and thou shalt glorify me (Psalm 50:14-15).[50]

Continue in prayer, and watch in the same with thanksgiving (Colossians 4:2).[51]

Giving thanks always for all things unto God and the Father in the name of our Lord Jesus Christ (Ephesians 5:20).[52]

Be not therefore anxious for the morrow; for the morrow will be anxious for itself. Sufficient unto the day is the evil thereof [Matthew 6:34—part of the Sermon on the Mount. (Quoted from the Revised Version)].[53]

---

[46] See Rose, *The Quiet Time*, p. 3; Fosdick, *The Meaning of Prayer*, p. 66; Winslow, *When I Awake*, p. 48; Tileston, *Daily Strength for Daily Needs*, p. 157; E. Stanley Jones, *Victorious Living*, p. 258; Dick B., *New Light on Alcoholism*, p. 44.

[47] Dick B., *New Light on Alcoholism*, p. 44, n. 12.

[48] See Tileston, *Daily Strength for Daily Needs*, p. 34; Fosdick, *The Meaning of Prayer*, p. 114.

[49] See Rose, *The Quiet Time*, p. 3; Holm, *The Runner's Bible*, p. 61; *The Upper Room*, for 6/13/35.

[50] Holm, *The Runner's Bible*, p. 38.

[51] See Holm, *The Runner's Bible*, p. 37; Tileston, *Daily Strength for Daily Needs*, p. 252; E. Stanley Jones, *Victorious Living*, p. 68.

[52] See Tileston, *Daily Strength for Daily Needs*, p. 88.

[53] Holm, *The Runner's Bible*, p. 41.

Be careful [anxious] for nothing; but in every thing by prayer and supplication with thanksgiving let your requests be made known unto God. And the peace of God which passeth all understanding, shall keep your hearts and minds through Christ Jesus (Philippians 4:6-7).[54]

Write Down the Thoughts That Come!

Thus speaketh the Lord God of Israel, saying, Write thee all the words that I have spoken unto thee in a book (Jeremiah 30:2).[55]

And the Lord answered me, and said, Write the vision, and make *it* plain upon tables, that he may run that readeth it (Habakkuk 2:2).[56]

Believe!

And all things, whatsoever ye shall ask in prayer, believing, ye shall receive (Matthew 21:22).[57]

Therefore I say unto you, what things soever ye desire, when ye pray, believe that ye receive *them*, and ye shall have *them* (Mark 11:24).[58]

And this is the confidence that we have in him, that, if we ask any thing according to his will, he heareth us: And if we know

---

[54] See Tileston, *Daily Strength for Daily Needs*, p. 53; Holm, *The Runner's Bible*, p. 61; E. Stanley Jones, *Victorious Living*, p. 137; Clark, *I Will Lift Up Mine Eyes*, p. 93; Fosdick, *The Meaning of Prayer*, p. 72; Roger Hick, *How to Read the Bible: Notes for Revolutionaries* (London: The Oxford Group, n.d.), p. 35.

[55] See Rose, *The Quiet Time*, p. 3; E. Stanley Jones, *Victorious Living*, p. 253; Hallen Viney, *How Do I Begin?* (The Oxford Group, 1937), p. 3.

[56] D. M. Prescott, *A New Day: Daily Readings for Our Time*, new ed. (London: Grosvenor Books, 1979), p. 31.

[57] Holm, *The Runner's Bible*, p. 42.

[58] Holm, *The Runner's Bible*, p. 42.

that he hear us, whatsoever we ask, we know that we have the petitions that we desired of him (1 John 5:14-15).[59]

It Works!

The effectual fervent prayer of a righteous man availeth much (James 5:16).[60]

―――――――――――

[59] Holm, *The Runner's Bible*, p. 64; Clark, *I Will Lift Up Mine Eyes*, p. 24; Dick B., *Design for Living*, p. 162.

[60] See Fosdick, *The Meaning of Prayer*, p. 158; Holm, *The Runner's Bible*, pp. 62, 114; *The Upper Room* for 8/19/35; Winslow, *When I Awake*, pp. 42-43; Hicks, *How to Read the Bible*, p. 35; Howard Walter, *Soul Surgery*, 6th ed. (Oxford at the University Press, John Johnson, 1940), p. 29; MacMillan, *Seeking and Finding*, p. 128; Dick B., *The Good Book and The Big Book*, pp. 102-03.

3

Listening through the Ages

This chapter is about "listening." In biblical terms, this means receiving revelation from God. Almost every quote is from materials read by Dr. Bob, Anne Smith, Henrietta Seiberling, T. Henry Williams, Clarace Williams, and the pioneer AAs. Or written by Dr. Sam Shoemaker or other Oxford Group people. And/or written or quoted in religious literature studied by early AAs. We will be looking at what religion had to say about the importance of listening to God and listening for messages from God—an "art" in the Oxford Group which found its way into page after page of A.A.'s Big Book.

The Classics

First, let's look at Saint Augustine, whose book, *The Confessions*, was owned, studied, and often quoted by early AAs and their progenitors. Augustine wrote:

> Thou awakest us to delight in Thy praise; for Thou madest us for Thyself, and our heart is restless, until it repose in Thee. Grant me, Lord, to know and understand which is first, to call on Thee or to praise Thee? and, again, to know Thee or to call on Thee? for who can call on Thee, not knowing Thee? for he that knoweth Thee not, may call on Thee as other than Thou art. Or,

is it rather, that we call on Thee that we may know Thee? but how shall they call on Him in whom they have not believed? or how shall they believe without a preacher? and they that seek the Lord shall praise Him: for they that seek shall find Him, and they that find shall praise Him. I will seek Thee, Lord, by calling on Thee; and will call Thee, believing in Thee; for to us hast Thou been preached. (Saint Augustine, 354-430 A.D.)[1]

Thomas à Kempis was also widely studied and quoted. He wrote:

"Speak, Lord, for Your servant listens." "I am Your servant; grant me understanding, that I may know Your testimonies." "Incline my heart to the words of Your mouth; let Your speech descend on me like the dew." The people of Israel of old time said to Moses, "Speak with us, and we will hear: let not God speak with us, lest we die." But I do not pray thus, O'Lord; but with the Prophet Samuel, I humbly and earnestly beg, "Speak Lord, for your servant listens." Let not Moses or any of the Prophets speak to me, but rather do You speak, O Lord God, who inspire and enlighten the Prophets. . . . The Prophets can preach the word, but they cannot bestow the Spirit. They speak most eloquently, but if You are silent, they cannot fire the heart. They instruct in the letter, but You open the understanding (Thomas à Kempis, 1380-1471 A.D.).[2]

In 1535, Martin Luther wrote the following which was quoted in one of the Oxford Group's earliest pieces of literature:

---

[1] *The Confessions of St. Augustine*, Cardinal ed. (New York: Pocket Books, Inc., 1952), p. 1. This book was owned and studied by Dr. Bob and frequently quoted by Oxford Group people, including Sam Shoemaker. See Dick B., *Dr. Bob's Library: Books for Twelve Step Growth* (San Rafael, CA: Paradise Research Publications, 1994), pp. 25-26; Samuel M. Shoemaker, Jr., *Religion That Works* (New York: Fleming H. Revell, 1928), p. 11; D. M. Prescott, *A New Day: Daily Readings for Our Time* new ed. (London: Grosvenor Books, 1979), p.167.

[2] Thomas à Kempis, *The Imitation of Christ* (London: Penguin Books, 1952), p. 92. See Dick B., *Dr. Bob's Library*, p. 26.

It so happens quite often that in contemplating on a part (of the Lord's Prayer) or one of the petitions, I come into such rich thoughts that I let all the other (petitions) alone. And when such rich and good thoughts come one ought to stop all other prayers and make room for such thoughts listening quietly and hindering them by no means. . . . And as I have said before about the Lord's Prayer I say again: In case the Holy Spirit should come among such thoughts and should begin to preach into your heart with rich and illuminating thoughts, then do homage to Him and let your own thoughts behind. Be still and listen to Him, who knows better than you. And keep in mind what He preaches and write it down. Then you will experience miracles.[3]

Saint Francis de Sales said:

Spend an hour every day, some time before the midday meal, in meditation; and the earlier the better, because your mind will then be less distracted, and fresh after a night's sleep (Saint Francis de Sales, 1567-1622 A.D.).[4]

Saint Vincent de Paul stated:

If they would resign themselves to outward silence, the souls of men would hear the voice of God (Saint Vincent de Paul, 1576-1660 A.D.).[5]

From the Preface to the 1611 (King James) Version of the Bible:

A blessed thing it is, and will bring us to everlasting blessedness in the end, when God speaketh unto us, to hearken; when He setteth His word before us, to read it; when He stretcheth out

---

[3] Eleanor Napier Forde (Newton), *The Guidance of God* (Great Britain: The Oxford Group, 1930), pp. 26-27.

[4] Prescott, *A New Day*, p. 1.

[5] Prescott, *A New Day*, p. 24.

His hand and calleth, to answer, Here am I, here we are to do Thy will, O God.[6]

Brother Lawrence had this to say, as quoted in *The Practice of the Presence of God*:

> When I first entered the monastery, I looked upon God as the beginning and the end of all my thoughts and all the feelings of my soul. During the hours designated for prayer, I meditated on the truth and character of God that we must accept by the light of faith, rather than spending time in laborious meditations and readings. . . . Completely immersed in my understanding of God's majesty, I used to shut myself up in the kitchen. There alone, after having done everything that was necessary for my work, I would devote myself to prayer in all the time that was left. . . . During my work, I would always continue to speak to the Lord as though He were right with me, offering Him my services and thanking Him for His assistance. And at the end of my work, I used to examine it carefully. If I found good in it, I thanked God. If I noticed faults, I asked His forgiveness without being discouraged, and then went on with my work still dwelling in Him. Thus, continuing in this practice of conversing with God throughout each day, and quickly seeking His forgiveness when I fell or strayed, His presence has become as easy and natural to me now as it once was difficult to attain (Brother Lawrence, 1611-1691 A.D.).[7]

From the 1800's Onward

In the last two centuries, some of A.A.'s source writers or writings have said the following:

> How do you change? By listening to God; because, as the sun is always shining, so God is constantly speaking. How do you

---

[6] Prescott, *A New Day*, p. 6

[7] Brother Lawrence, *The Practice of the Presence of God* (Springdale, PA; Whitaker House, 1982), pp. 81-83; Dick B., *Dr. Bob's Library*, pp. 26-27.

listen to God? The best time is in the morning, before all distractions and activities intervene. How can you listen to God, you ask me? This is the answer: you write. Write, so that you may better hear the Word that is in you and keep His instructions (Pere Gratry, 1805-1872).[8]

Two-way Prayer: God gave a man two ears and only one mouth. Why don't we listen twice as much as we talk. . . . *Write It Down*: The strongest memory is weaker than the palest ink (two Chinese proverbs).[9]

If it were not for my firm belief in an over-ruling Providence, it would be difficult for me, in the midst of such complications of affairs, to keep my reason in its seat. (But) I have so many evidences of God's direction that I cannot doubt this power comes from above. I am satisfied that when the Almighty wants me to do or not to do any particular thing, He finds a way of letting me know it (Abraham Lincoln, 1809-1865).[10]

God's law and His written Word are guides to present duty, which, if faithfully accepted, will help you in accordance with the mind of God and the plan He has laid for you. "I am a stranger in the earth," said one; "hide not Thy commandments from me;" knowing that God's commandments would give him a clue to the true meaning and business of his life. . . . Go to God himself, and ask for the calling of God; for, as certainly as He has a plan or calling for you, He will somehow guide you into it. And this is the proper office and work of His Spirit. By this private teaching He can shew us, and will, into the very plan

---

[8] Prescott, *A New Day*, p. 31.

[9] Prescott, *A New Day*, pp. 29-31. See also Dick B., *That Amazing Grace: The Role of Clarence and Grace S. in Alcoholics Anonymous* (San Rafael, CA: Paradise Research Publications, 1996), p. 88; Samuel M. Shoemaker, Jr., *The Conversion of the Church* (New York: Fleming H. Revell, 1932), p. 60; Cecil Rose, *When Man Listens* (New York: Oxford University Press, 1937), p. 37; Howard C. Blake: *Way to Go: Adventures in Search of God's Will* (Merrifield, VA: Pooh Stix Press, 1992), pp. 66-67.

[10] Prescott, *A New Day*, p. 27; K. D. Belden, *Moral Re-Armament* (London: Grosvenor Books, 1979), pp. 24-25.

that is set for us . . . for the Spirit of God is a kind of universal presence, or inspiration, in the world's bosom; an unfailing inner light, which, if we accept and live in, we are guided thereby into a consenting choice, so that what God wills for us we also will for ourselves . . . By this hidden union with God, or intercourse with Him, we get a wisdom, or insight deeper than we know ourselves. . . . (Horace Bushnell).[11]

[T]he ideal man . . . must speak to his Friend. He cannot be silent in such company. And speaking to such a Friend is not mere conversation. It has a higher name. It is communion. It is prayer. . . . Everyone remembers the words of the ideal prayer: "Thy will be Done" (Matt. vi.10). . . . What does he want from the great Teacher? . . . "Teach me to do Thy Will" (Psalm 143:10). . . . There is God's will dropped softly on the believer's ear in angel whispers or the still small voice of God. . . . Now this region may be distinguished from other regions. For one thing, by its *secrecy*. It is a private thing; between God and you. You want to know what to do next. . . . Then you enter into this private chamber of God's will, and ask the private question, "Lord, what wouldest thou have *me* to do (Professor Henry Drummond, Evangelist and Oxford Group mentor)?"[12]

The Psalms are full of earnest pleadings for clear direction: "Show me thy way, O Lord, lead me in a plain path, because of mine enemies."[13] It is the law of our Father's house that His children shall ask for what they want. "If any man lack wisdom, let him ask of God, who giveth to all men liberally, and upbraideth not."[14] In a time of change and crisis, we need to be much in prayer, not only on our knees, but in that sweet form of inward prayer, in which the spirit is constantly offering itself up to God, asking to be shown His will. . . . One good form of

---

[11] Horace Bushnell, *The New Life* (London: Strahan & Co., 1868), p. 11.

[12] Henry Drummond, *The Ideal Life: Addresses Hitherto Unpublished* (New York: Hodder & Stoughton, 1897), pp. 236-37, 240, 278-79.

[13] Cp. Ps. 27:11.

[14] Cp. James 1:5.

prayer at such a juncture is to ask that doors be shut, that the way be closed, and that all enterprises which are not according to God's will may be arrested at their very beginning. Put the matter absolutely into God's hands from the out-set. . . . I would encourage each troubled and perplexed soul that may read these lines to wait patiently for the Lord, until He clearly indicates His will (Congregational Minister F. B. Meyer).[15]

If you wish to make your life effective and useful for God and your fellow-men, it is essential that you should put aside unhurried time every day for a morning watch with God (Dr. John R. Mott of Student Christian Movement and YMCA fame).[16]

Words from Two of Bill W.'s Friends in the Clergy

For meditation the ear of the soul is more important than the tongue; St. Paul tells us that faith comes from listening. Most people commit the same mistake with God that they do with their friends; they do all the talking. Our Lord warned us against those who "use many phrases like the heathen, who think to make themselves heard by their eloquence" (Matt. 6:7). One can be impolite to God, too, by absorbing all the conversation, and by changing the words of the Scripture from "Speak, Lord, Thy servant hears" to "Listen, Lord, Thy servant speaks." God has things to tell us which will enlighten us—we must wait for Him to speak. No one would rush into a physicians's office, rattle off his symptoms, then dash away again without waiting for a diagnosis; no one would tune in the radio and immediately leave the room. It is every bit as stupid to ring God's doorbell and then run away (Bishop Fulton J. Sheen).[17]

---

[15] F. B. Meyer, *The Secret of Guidance* (New York: Fleming H. Revell, 1896), pp. 11-12, 14, 18.

[16] See quote in Jack C. Winslow, *When I Awake: Thoughts on Keeping of the Morning Watch* (London: Hodder & Stoughton, 1938), p. 9.

[17] Quoted in Prescott, *A New Day*, p. 29.

One of our strongest misconceptions concerning prayer is that it consists chiefly in our *talking* to God, whereas the best part of prayer is our *listening* to God. Sometimes in the Scripture a prayer of urgent and definite petition rises, "Oh that I might have my request; And that God would grant me the thing that I long for!" (Job 6:8); but another sort of prayer is very frequently indicated: "Speak; for thy servant heareth" (I Sam. 3:10); "My soul, wait thou in silence for God only; For my expectation is from him" (Psalm 62:5); "I will hear what God Jehovah will speak" (Psalm 85:8); or in Luther's version of Psalm 37:7, "Be silent to God and let him mold thee." Without such openheartedness to God, some things which he wills never can be done (A.A.'s early friend, Dr. Harry Emerson Fosdick).[18]

A Child's Song

The following song is frequently used with the children and others in the author's own Bible fellowship in Hawaii:

> God has something to say to you.
> God has something to say.
> Listen, listen.
> Pay close attention.
> God has something to say.

---

[18] Harry Emerson Fosdick, *The Meaning of Prayer* (New York: Association Press, 1934), p. 66. This Fosdick title was recommended for reading by Dr. Bob's wife, Anne Ripley Smith. See Dick B., *Anne Smith's Journal, 1933-1939: A.A.'s Principles of Success* (San Rafael, CA: Paradise Research Publications, 1995), p. 82. Note that Fosdick endorsed the First Edition of A.A.'s Big Book.

4

Quiet Time Roots

The Oxford Group

As a young man of thirty, the Reverend Frank N. D. Buchman (the Oxford Group's founder-to-be) was asked to serve as YMCA Secretary at Pennsylvania State College. During his tenure in that post, he met the famous evangelist F. B. Meyer. The following colloquy occurred:

> Meyer . . . asked, "Do you let the Holy Spirit guide you in all you are doing?" Buchman replied that he did indeed pray and read the Bible in the morning and sometimes received inspirations then and at other times in the day. "But," persisted Meyer, "do you give God enough uninterrupted time really to tell you what to do?"[1]

Meyer often expressed such views on "listening." For example, he wrote:

---

[1] From Garth Lean, *On the Tail of a Comet: The Life of Frank Buchman, a Small Town American Who Awakened the Conscience of the World* (Colorado Springs: Helmers & Howard, 1988), pp. 35-36.

It is not necessary to make long prayers, but it is essential to be much alone with God; waiting at His door; hearkening for His voice; lingering in the garden of Scripture for the coming of the Lord God in the dawn or cool of the day. No number of meetings, no fellowship with Christian friends, no amount of Christian activity can compensate for the neglect of the still hour.[2]

Obey exactly and immediately the commands of the inner still small voice. It can be recognized by the fact that it never alters, never asks questions, but is always direct and explicit. Often it asks for an obedience which is against, or above, what we might naturally feel disposed to give. Listen to that still small voice—the voice of the Spirit of God. . . .[3]

Buchman was motivated to change as a result of hearing Meyer. He made a decision to give at least an hour each day in the early morning to listening to God, a period which Buchman came to refer to as a "quiet time."[4]

Buchman also received quiet time inspiration from Professor Henry B. Wright of Yale University. At the time of his early acquaintance with Buchman, Wright was Assistant Professor of Latin History and Literature at Yale. Buchman had been much encouraged by contact with Professor Wright and by studying Wright's book, *The Will of God and a Man's Lifework*, which was published in 1909.[5] Wright later was appointed to a special chair in Christian Methods at Yale Divinity School; and Wright visited Buchman each year to aid Buchman in his work with students at Pennsylvania State University. Still later, Buchman, Wright, and an American evangelist, Howard A. Walter, collaborated on the

---

[2] F. B. Meyer, *The Secret of Guidance* (New York: Fleming H. Revell, 1896), pp. 28-29.

[3] F. B. Meyer, *Five Musts* (Chicago: Moody Press, 1927), p. 107.

[4] Lean, *On the Tail of a Comet*, p. 36.

[5] Henry B. Wright, *The Will of God and a Man's Lifework* (New York: The Young Men's Christian Association Press, 1909).

writing of a book, called *Soul Surgery*, which became a foundational work on Buchman/Oxford Group life-changing methods.[6]

Oxford Group writer and long-time Buchman associate T. Willard Hunter observed, as to Buchman and Wright: "The Yale professor [Wright] was probably the most influential single individual in Frank's entire life, outside his mother."[7] Buchman's biographer concluded:

> The central theme of Wright's book (*The Will of God*) was that an individual could, through "two-way prayer"—listening for guidance as well as talking—find God's will for his life and for the ordinary events of the day. Wright himself set aside half an hour for such listening prayer first thing every morning. At such times—and indeed at any time in the day—he declared that what he called "luminous thoughts" came from God, provided only that the human receiver was clean enough to pick them up. These thoughts Wright wrote down in a notebook and always tried to carry out.[8]

At one point, Buchman was journeying from Hartford Theological Seminary to Yale regularly (four hours there and back) simply to hear Wright's lectures. Wright's two-way prayer practices certainly coincided with those Buchman espoused. And Buchman

---

[6] Howard A. Walter, *Soul Surgery: Some Thoughts on Incisive Personal Work*, 6th ed. (Oxford at the University Press by John Johnson, 1940). In an author's note set forth in the Sixth Edition, Walter was quoted as follows: "For much of the general background of ideas in this pamphlet I am indebted to Professor Henry Wright, of Yale Divinity School, and Dr. Frank N. D. Buchman, of Hartford Theological Seminary, who acknowledge their own vast debt to the pioneer in this field, Henry Drummond. Those who are aware of the very wide and rich experience of Dr. Wright and Dr. Buchman as personal evangelists, are waiting with eagerness for the volume on this theme upon which they are collaborating."

[7] T. Willard Hunter, *World Changing Through Life Changing*, Thesis, Newton Center, Massachusetts; Andover-Newton Theological School, 1977, pp. 15-16.

[8] Lean, *On the Tail of a Comet*, p. 74.

once wrote Wright from China saying, "Much of the best in my message is due to you."[9]

Buchman took the position that communing with God had been the practice of the saints down through the ages; and he believed anyone could have such contact. In 1920, he sent Sam Shoemaker a seven-page letter citing Scriptural and theological authority for his thesis. Buchman said:

> This listening to God is not the experience of a few men. It's the most sane, normal, healthful thing a person can do. . . . I am absolutely convinced from my clinical reactions both at Princeton and in other places that it is possible for babes in Christ to have this experience.[10]

B. H. Streeter, the distinguished Oxford University theologian, became one of Buchman's colleagues and supporters. And Streeter wrote the following in *The God Who Speaks*:

> There is an inner coherence between the conception of God's plan and the two convictions—that conscience is the "voice of God", and that certain intuitions, which come to the individual with an imperative quality, may be interpreted as "divine guidance." . . . I will only suggest that in the phenomenon of prophecy we find, in its highest and most intensified form, that conviction of direct communication between human and divine which appears also in the belief that conscience is the voice of God and that divine guidance is a possibility in normal experience (p. 15).

> Popular Christianity, however, has inclined to forget that Christ said: "But when ye pray, use not vain repetitions, as the heathen do: for they think that they shall be heard for their much speaking. Be not ye therefore like unto them: for your Father knoweth what things ye have need of, before ye ask him" (Mt.

---

[9] Theophil Spoerri, *Dynamic out of Silence: Frank Buchman's Relevance Today* (London: Grosvenor Books, 1976), p. 39.

[10] Lean, *On the Tail of a Comet*, p. 75.

vi.7-8). It would seem, then, to accord well with Christ's teaching that, whenever possible, we should begin the day by attuning the soul to the contemplation of the Divine (by some act of aspiration, or by the reading of scripture or other noble words) and should then, before offering any petitions of personal needs, wait in silence—listening, if haply the inner voice should bring some guidance, some indication of the part in God's plan which the worshipper may be called upon to play that day. Often to those who listen so there comes a thought or word, clear and definite, pointing to action (pp. 18-19).[11]

Eleanor Napier Forde has been a tireless worker for the Oxford Group from the 1920's to the date of this writing. She married Oxford Group activist James Draper Newton; and she was a friend of, and co-worker with, Oxford Group founder, Dr. Frank Buchman, and Buchman's chief American lieutenant, the Reverend Samuel M. Shoemaker. In 1930, Eleanor Forde's Oxford Group pamphlet, *The Guidance of God*, was published. She wrote:

We turn to think of God's Presence in the quiet time. We take for granted the fact that He is always with us. One has but to read the inspiring memoirs of Brother Lawrence . . . or recall the Jongleur de Dieu, turning his somersaults to the glory of God, to realize this. That he can hearten us, walking along the street, or see that we are in a given place at the right moment goes without saying. The reason why the quiet time is of supreme importance is that there we can shut out the world with its clamour of duty, its conflicting appeals, and our own tangled thoughts, and realize the presence of God—"the ineffable something that holds the mind.". . . The quiet time is not to bring that world into touch with us, but to carry us out of ourselves, beyond its frontier, where our spirits may be swept by the Spirit of worship and wonder, which is the very climate of the Unseen. . . . The purpose of quiet time, then, is not primarily to obtain direction but to come into the stillness—"that greatest and most awful of all goods which we can fancy," where

---

[11] Burnett Hillman Streeter, *The God Who Speaks* (London: Macmillan & Co., 1943).

God can find and commune with us. We need time enough to
forget time, and this often means the sacrifice of other interests
and almost inevitably that last precious hour of morning sleep.
It is not too much to say that for many people the power of the
whole day completely depends on that first hour alone with God,
and the man who would move mountains must have given God
his ear before the rush of life is upon him.[12]

Shortly after the Forde pamphlet was published, A. J. Russell's
popular *For Sinners Only* appeared on the scene.[13] Russell's title
contained the personal stories of Oxford Group adherents, laid out
Oxford Group principles, and captured the loyalty for the Group
of A. J. Russell himself, the book's author. Russell's book was
widely studied and included such readers as A.A.'s Dr. Bob and
Dr. Bob's wife Anne, who recommended the book to early AAs
and their families. As to quiet time, Russell wrote:

Here I had my first practical experience of the Quiet Time, a
first principle of the Group and one of the biggest obstacles to
the newcomer, but a principle on which the Group can make no
compromise. Guidance must come to all those who surrender to
God's will. As Ken Twitchell announced the Quiet Time the
undergraduates fumbled for pencils and guidance-books and
began to "listen in" to God. This was not simple meditation,
which may be concentration on some aspect of Christ or the
Gospel, but something more: a listening for definite messages
applicable to present needs. As they were committed to doing
God's will, that will could be known for them at any moment of
necessity (p. 93).

The Group said the individual was guided by God both during
Quiet Time and throughout the day in the following ways:
Through the Holy Spirit in attentive prayer by means of: The
Scriptures. The Conscience. Luminous Thoughts. Cultivating the

[12] Eleanor Napier Forde, *The Guidance of God* (Oxford: The Oxford Group, 1930),
pp. 23-24.

[13] A. J. Russell, *For Sinners Only* (London: Hodder & Stoughton, 1932).

Mind of Christ. Through reading the Bible and prayer. Through circumstances. Through reason. Through Church, Group, or Fellowship (p. 94).

Jack C. Winslow was a prolific Oxford Group writer on Oxford Group principles.[14] Winslow's writings were recommended in Sam Shoemaker's *Calvary Evangel*. And, in 1938, Winslow wrote a title, *When I Awake*, which bore this statement on its cover: "This book deals with the time of private prayer which it is essential all Christians should keep, morning by morning, if they desire to go forward in the Christian life."[15] Winslow wrote:

> I am constantly asked to give, or find myself needing to give, simple instruction about how to keep what some call a "quiet time" and others a "morning watch" with God. . . . I am dealing here solely with the time of private prayer which it is essential all Christians should keep, morning by morning, if they desire to go forward in the Christian life. . . , there is the great debt I owe to the Oxford Group, through which I have learnt much during the last few years, particularly with regard to what I have called "the prayer of attention," and the waiting upon God with confident expectation for definite and concrete guidance (pp. 5-6).

> If we want power in our own lives—victory over the things that get us down, and the invigorating sense of adequacy for any tasks or situations that await us through the day—we must let the Spirit of God re-charge us morning by morning (p. 12).

> The morning watch with God is also the surest guarantee of progress. . . . If I appear to stand exactly where I did a year ago, it must mean that I have been missing all those things which

---

[14] See, for example, Jack C. Winslow, *Why I Believe in the Oxford Group* (London: Hodder & Stoughton, 1934).

[15] Jack C. Winslow, *When I Awake: Thoughts on the Keeping of the Morning Watch* (London: Hodder & Stoughton, 1938).

God was waiting to teach and give me. In my own experience
this kind of stagnation is most often due to the fact that my quiet
times with God have become formal and uncreative. On the other
hand, if I can really say with the prophet (Isaiah 1:4), "Morning
by morning He wakeneth mine ear to hear as they that are
taught," then I find that I begin at once to go forward. I grow in
understanding of God as I meditate on the Bible. I get fresh
glimpses of His character, His purposes, the ways of His
working (p. 13).

Since I learnt morning by morning to commit the day to God, to
try to see His plan for each day so far as He chose to show it,
and to wait for whatever orders He might wish to give me, life
has had for me a thrill and a purpose such as it never had before.
. . . The quiet hour with God in the early morning is also a sure
secret of inward peace. . . . I have risen from bed with a sense
of anxiety or worry—perhaps troubled about definite problems
for which I could see no solution; perhaps haunted by that vague
sense of depression about nothing in particular which so many
experience in the early morning. I have entered on my quiet tryst
with God, and in the stillness, as I have committed myself with
all my anxieties to God, peace has stolen back into my soul (pp.
14-15).

The stress on this watch with God as the *morning* watch is of
vital importance. . . . It is the time when we are most free from
distractions. . . . The early morning is also the time when our
minds should be at their freshest. . . . There is something in our
psychological make-up which makes us peculiarly susceptible to
deeper intuitions in our first minutes of re-awakened
consciousness (pp. 17-18).

In March, 1935, during a speech to 35,000 people at Hamlet's
Castle in Denmark, Dr. Frank Buchman summed up what he
believed to be the importance of his ideas on listening for the
guidance of God. In graphic terms that were frequently repeated
thereafter, even in part by Bill Wilson's wife Lois in her Oxford

Group notes which the author inspected at the Wilson Home in New York, Buchman said:

> By a miracle of science millions can think and feel as one. Barriers of time and space are swept away. A commonwealth of many nations and languages becomes a family. Radio listeners understand that miracle. And they will also understand the Oxford Group, which is showing people how to listen in to God. "God calling the world" is becoming a daily experience in the lives of hundreds and thousands of people in the more than fifty countries where the Oxford Group is at work. We accept as commonplace a man's voice carried by radio to the uttermost parts of the earth. Why not the voice of the living God as an active, creative force in every home, every business, every parliament? Men listen to a king when he speaks to people over the air. Why not to the King of Kings? He is alive, and constantly broadcasting. . . . The Holy Spirit is the most intelligent source of information in the world today. He has the answer to every problem. Everywhere when men will let Him, He is teaching them how to live. . . . Divine guidance must become the normal experience of ordinary men and women. Any man can pick up divine messages if he will put his receiving set in order. Definite, accurate, adequate information can come from the Mind of God to the minds of men. This is normal prayer.[16]

Thoughts of Bill W.'s Teacher and Friend, Sam Shoemaker

Dr. Shoemaker began explaining and pleading for morning prayer and meditation in the very first of his significant published titles. Like so many religious leaders of his day, Shoemaker first called morning prayer time the "Morning Watch." In *Realizing Religion*, he wrote:

---

[16] Frank N. D. Buchman, *Remaking the World* (London: Blandford Press, 1961), pp. 11-12.

Frances R. Havergal said long ago that the reason the churches lacked power was that so few Christians were spending the first hour of the day alone with God. "Our sense of perceptions of all kinds," says Dr. Henry Churchill King, "are far acuter in the morning." One could name literally hundreds of great spiritual leaders who have considered this the most luminous and precious and indispensable hour of the day, as the study of their lives will make plain to anyone. This practice of the "Morning Watch" is the most fruitful personal habit of religion for those who use it; and were you to draw a line between the strong and the weak Christians, you would find, I believe, the cultivation or neglect of this chief source of their difference in power. It takes dogged will to choose with unbroken regularity half an hour—less is almost too brief a time to "get into the spirit" of it—the first thing every day. But the results will justify the effort; and granted the desire and determination to use this time daily, with the Bible open before you, you will soon make a method of study for yourself that will suit you better than anything which this book might recommend (pp. 60-61).[17]

If the reader will pardon a personal testimony, the time when the writer began to have a hitherto unknown power in his own life, and some slight influence spiritually in the lives of others, coincides exactly with the time when he changed the chief time of prayer from the last thing at night to the first thing in the morning. I plead again for the keeping of the "Morning Watch"—coming fresh to God with the daily plans unmade, submitting first our spirits and then our duties to Him for the shedding of His white light upon both. "To start full-speed through icebergs is irreligious. To start the day without one thought of our Maker is to invite catastrophe" (pp. 65-66).

By the time he was writing *Religion That Works* just a few years later, Shoemaker was most eloquently championing the guided life. He said:

---

[17] Samuel M. Shoemaker, Jr., *Realizing Religion* (New York: Association Press, 1923).

I believe enormously in the possibility of a guided life, influenced and led at every step by the Holy Spirit. Conversion is the beginning, not the ending of an experience of God. That experience continues when we use all the means Jesus put at our disposal for continuation—prayer, the Scriptures, the Church and the Sacraments, Christian fellowship and worship. . . . Many situations in my life are not covered by the Sermon on the Mount. I need special guidance and illumination. The prophets of Israel had it. The apostles had it. Where is it gone to in this age? We believe in the Holy Spirit as we believe in some dead human character: he was once, but he is gone. The deepest need of our age, the cure for most of our back-door attempts to establish communication with the other worlds, is a rediscovery of the Holy Spirit. What infinite possibilities of learning the will of God, through communion with Him, may lie ahead of us, who can dare to imagine? (pp. 14-15).[18]

Still later, Shoemaker expanded upon the availability of guidance and upon the time or times for obtaining it. At this point, however, Shoemaker preferred to call the period for communion with God his "Quiet Time." In *The Conversion of the Church,* he wrote:

We want to know that God can and does speak directly to the human heart. The reason why some of us believe in guidance, at least in theory, is that the Old and New Testaments are full of instances of it, specific as you please. Men said clearly that they were guided of God in this and that act and decision. You may try to psychologize all this away if you want; but I prefer to see whether this sort of thing is not now possible to those who put their trust in God entirely (p. 50).[19]

---

[18] Samuel M. Shoemaker, Jr., *Religion That Works* (New York: Fleming H. Revell, 1928).

[19] Samuel M. Shoemaker, Jr., *The Conversion of the Church* (New York: Fleming H. Revell, 1932).

How, then, shall we seek this inspiration from the Holy Spirit, till His slightest motion is our ready desire? I can only speak from my own experience. Something happened to the quality of my time of prayer when I moved up out of the old conception of a "Morning Watch" (which had a way of slipping round till evening), to the conception of a "Quiet Time." The emphasis was in a different place. Formerly I had sought to find my way up to God. Now I let Him find His way down to me. Listening became the dominant note. Not the exclusive note; for there was Bible study first, taking a book and studying it straight through; there was ordinary prayer, confession, petition, thanksgiving, intercession. But the bulk of the time is listening. Most of us find it indispensable to have a loose-leaf note-book, in which to write down the things which come to us. It goes without saying that such a period is best in the early morning, while the body and mind are fresh and rested, the perceptions clear and unclouded, and the day is before us. We shall want to stop more than once in the day for further direction, especially with others about problems which concern them and us. But nothing makes up for our own private time alone with the living God" (pp. 59-61).

As an aside, the author would point out that he was privileged to examine Shoemaker's personal journals for the period 1931 to 1936. Shoemaker's daughters made this possible. And the journals were just as described by Shoemaker in his books. They were voluminous in content. They were hand-written. They were contained in small loose-leafed ringed binders. And they were detailed in their references to Scripture, to Shoemaker's colleagues and family, to dates and plans and places, and to inspirational thoughts concerning each of these.

Ye Must Be Born Again!

Before we get to the *specifics* of quiet time practices among A.A.'s root sources, it is essential to review what those sources believed was the condition precedent to receiving *any guidance at all.*[20]

In his first title, Sam Shoemaker was careful to point out where people must start. Shoemaker said:

> Now St. Augustine said truly: "We are not born Christians, but we become Christians (p. 5)."[21]

> What you want is simply a vital religious experience. You need to find God. You need Jesus Christ (p. 9).

> God on His part has longed to win us for years. It has been we who have been unwilling. We must open ourselves to Him, and be prepared to accept all that it will mean to be a child of God (pp. 28-29).

In answer to certain objections, Shoemaker wrote:

> The world does not need an awakening any more than the Church does. It was to an educated religious gentleman [Nicodemus] that Jesus said, "Ye must be born again." That imperative is a judgment against those who withstand conversion. But it is a hope held out to those fearful and self-depreciating people who do not think themselves capable of conversion.[22]

---

[20] For some preliminary thoughts on Oxford Group understanding of the importance of 1 Corinthians, Chapter 2, and of being born again of God's spirit in order to discern spiritual matters, see Streeter, *The God Who Speaks*, p. 110; Benson, *The Eight Points of the Oxford Group*, p. 79.

[21] Shoemaker, *Realizing Religion*, p. 5.

[22] Shoemaker, *Religion That Works*, p. 14; *Children of the Second Birth* (New York: Fleming H. Revell, 1927), p. 32.

Jesus Christ said the following to Nicodemus in John 3:

> Verily, verily, I say unto thee, Except a man be born again, he
> cannot see the kingdom of God. . . . Verily, verily, I say unto
> thee, Except a man be born of water and *of* the Spirit, he cannot
> enter into the kingdom of God. That which is born of the flesh
> is flesh; and that which is born of the Spirit is spirit. Marvel not
> that I said unto thee, Ye must be born again. The wind bloweth
> where it listeth, and thou hearest the sound thereof, but canst not
> tell whence it cometh, and whither it goeth: so is every one that
> is born of the Spirit (John 3:3, 5-8).

The Book of Acts records the following concerning Paul's trip to
Ephesus:

> He [Paul] said unto them, Have ye received the Holy Ghost since
> ye believed? And they said unto him, We have not so much as
> heard whether there be any Holy Ghost. And he said unto them,
> Unto what then were ye baptized? And they said, Unto John's
> baptism. Then said Paul, John verily baptized with the baptism
> of repentance, saying unto the people, that they should believe
> on him which should come after him, that is, on Christ Jesus.
> When they heard *this*, they were baptized in the name of the
> Lord Jesus. And when Paul had laid *his* hands upon them, the
> Holy Ghost came on them; and they spake with tongues, and
> prophesied (Acts 19:1-6).

As she so often did in her sharing with early AAs and their
families, Dr. Bob's wife Anne Ripley Smith stressed the need for
a "receiving set," for "power," in order to be saved, made
complete, receive revelation, and be set free.[23] Anne wrote:

> Paul speaks of a wish toward good, but power to carry it out is
> lacking. A stronger power than his was needed. God provided
> the power through Christ, so that we could find a new kind of

---

[23] Cp. Romans 10:9; 1 Corinthians 12:7-11; John 8:31, 32; Matthew 22:29.

relationship with God. Christ gives the power, we appropriate it. It is not anything that we do ourselves; but it is the appropriation of a power that comes from God that saves us from sin and sets us free.[24]

A.A. pioneer Clarence S. pointed out that he had been given a verse in his earliest A.A. days—a verse that changed his life.[25] The verse was 2 Corinthians 5:17:

Therefore if any man *be* in Christ, *he is* a new creature: old things are passed away; behold, all things are become new.[26]

The Apostle Peter explained the change which Clarence S. experienced at the time of his rebirth:

Being born again, not of corruptible seed, but of incorruptible, by the word of God, which liveth and abideth forever (1 Peter 1:23).[27]

Oxford Group writer K. D. Belden pointed out:

That is why we need a Saviour: to save us from ourselves, not just our actions. Only the Power which raised Jesus Christ from

---

[24] See Dick B., *Anne Smith's Journal, 1933-1939: A.A.'s Principles of Success* (San Rafael, CA: Paradise Research Publications, 1995), pp. 22-24.

[25] Dick B., *That Amazing Grace: The Role of Clarence and Grace S. in Alcoholics Anonymous* (San Rafael, CA: Paradise Research Publications, 1996), pp. 33-34.

[26] See also Streeter, *The God Who Speaks*, p. 111; Howard C. Blake, *Way to Go: Adventures in Search of God's Will* (Merrifield, VA: Pooh Stix Press, 1992), p. 79.

[27] Clarence explained a number of times that he had been born again at the home of T. Henry Williams in Akron. See Dick B., *That Amazing Grace*, pp. 16, 27-28, 52, 68, 83-84, 92-93. The nature of the change is described in Clarence's all-important verse, 2 Corinthians 5:17—Clarence was a new man in Christ. The reason for the change is explained in 1 Peter 1:23—that he had been born again of incorruptible seed (the seed of Christ).

the dead can, and will, raise us from our old nature and begin to form in us the new.[28]

The early AAs in Akron were very clear that they were Christians—"A Christian Fellowship."[29] Dr. Bob frequently told his business friends that the alcoholic squad of the Oxford Group were "a Christian Fellowship."[30] The Oxford Group itself was called "A First Century Christian Fellowship" during the 1920's and early 1930's.[31] And there seems to have been general agreement as to A.A.'s Christian leanings in the earliest days; for Bill Wilson told a story in his last major address to AAs in 1969 that showed how "membership" issues and "religious affiliation" were resolved by Dr. Bob in connection with a particular membership "applicant." Bill said:

> Finally, there was some kind of hearing on it [the issue of the man's "membership"] among the self-appointed elders. I remember how perfectly Bob put it to them. He reminded us that most of us were practicing Christians. Then he asked, "What would the Master have thought? Would He have kept this man away?" He had them cold! The man came in, was a prodigious worker, and was one of our most respected people.[32]

---

[28] K. D. Belden, *Reflections on Moral Re-Armament* (London: Grosvenor Books, 1983), p. 42.

[29] Dick B., *The Good Book and The Big Book: A.A.'s Roots in the Bible* (San Rafael, CA: Paradise Research Publications, 1995), pp. 13-14. For precise details, and Bill Wilson's own words concerning his "born again" experience, see Dick B., *The Akron Genesis of Alcoholics Anonymous* (Corte Madera, CA: Good Book Publishing Company, 1994), pp. 328-31; *New Light on Alcoholism: The A.A. Legacy from Sam Shoemaker* (Corte Madera, CA: Good Book Publishing Company, 1994), pp. 55-56.

[30] See Dick B., *The Akron Genesis*, pp. 187-88; *Design for Living: The Oxford Group's Contribution to Early A.A.* (San Rafael, CA: Paradise Research Publications, 1995), p. 85; *DR. BOB and the Good Oldtimers* (New York: Alcoholics Anonymous World Services, 1980), p. 118.

[31] Dick B., *Design for Living*, pp. 83-85; *Pass It On* (New York: Alcoholics Anonymous World Services, 1984), p. 130.

[32] *The Co-Founders of Alcoholics Anonymous: Biographical Sketches: Their Last Major Talks* (New York: Alcoholics Anonymous World Services, 1972, 1975), p. 30.

But the important thing, in examining the roots of "quiet time," "listening," "revelation," and "guidance," is the need to understand that Oxford Group people emphasized *surrender to God* and the relationship with God *as the first pre-requisite to receiving God's guidance.* First, one surrendered, became converted, or "gave his life to God." Then that person sought guidance from his or her Heavenly Father. It was not the other way around. Sam Shoemaker, for example, was famous for getting people on their knees before he began his work to help them change their lives with God's help.[33] Frank Buchman was well-known for his declaration, "Sin, Jesus Christ, and (the result) a Miracle."[34] The approach was not the other way around.

The Oxford Group people had their own way of effecting a conversion or surrender. Commonly, it involved the *"manage me" prayer.* The prayer, with slight variations, was "O, God, manage me, because I cannot manage myself!" For those closely allied with Oxford Group founder Frank Buchman, the prayer became known in connection with a boy Frank Buchman met in the Himalayas. The boy's name was "Victor." When the boy surrendered, Frank Buchman told him to give all of himself that he knew to all that he knew of God. And the two got on their

---

[33] See how it all began in China as recounted by Sam Shoemaker in the chapter entitled "The Turning Point" in *Faith at Work: A Symposium Edited by Samuel Moor Shoemaker* (n.p.: Hawthorne Books, 1958), pp. 80-84. See also the accounts in Samuel M. Shoemaker, Jr., *Children of the Second Birth* (New York: Fleming H. Revell, 1927), pp. 122-23, 148, 171, 178. Years later, Shoemaker was still getting people on their knees surrendering their lives to God. See accounts in Duncan Norton-Taylor, "Businessmen on Their Knees," *Fortune*, October, 1953; "Pittsburgh Steels Itself for 2000," *For A Change*, August-September, 1994, pp. 8-9; and Michael J. Sider, *Taking the Gospel to the Point: Evangelicals in Pittsburgh and the Origins of the Pittsburgh Leadership Foundation* (Pittsburgh: Pittsburgh Leadership Foundation, n.d.), pp. 5-12.

[34] See H. A. Walter, *Soul Surgery: Some Thoughts on Incisive Personal Work*, 6th ed. (London: Blandford Press, n.d.), p. 86; Harry J. Almond, *Foundations for Faith*, 2d ed. (London: Grosvenor Books, 1980), pp. 10-29.

knees where the boy said, "Lord, manage me, for I can't manage myself."[35]

In Sam Shoemaker's circles, the prayer was often known as "Charlie's prayer." It took its name from the prayer of a young Italian newsboy named Charlie, whom Sam Shoemaker met in Gramercy Park. Charlie received new life when he uttered the prayer, "God, manage me, 'cause I can't manage myself."[36] And Dr. Bob's wife, Anne, three times utilized this prayer in the spiritual journal she kept and read to early AAs.[37]

For many early AAs, the prerequisite surrender apparently involved saying the "Sinners Prayer."[38] For some, the very clear salvation mandate of Romans 10:9-10 was not overlooked. Romans 10:9 states: "That if thou shalt confess with thy mouth the Lord Jesus, and shalt believe in thine heart that God hath raised him from the dead, thou shalt be saved." Shoemaker and other A.A. sources did refer to this mandate, but with surprising infrequency.[39]

As we discuss the receipt of revelation from God (or "guidance," as the Oxford Group called it), it is important to note that, according to the Bible, an unbeliever does not receive

---

[35] See Dick B., *Design for Living*, pp. 77-78. The "Victor" surrender story was told innumerable times in connection with the "manage me" prayer. See Lean, *On the Tail of a Comet*, pp. 47-48; Spoerri, *Dynamic out of Silence*, pp. 34-37; Russell, *For Sinners Only*, p. 79; Cecil Rose, *When Man Listens* (New York: Oxford University Press, 1937), pp. 19-22; Peter Howard, *Frank Buchman's Secret* (New York: Doubleday & Company, 1961), pp. 41-44.

[36] Dick B., *New Light on Alcoholism: The A.A. Legacy from Sam Shoemaker* (Corte Madera, CA: Good Book Publishing Company, 1994), pp. 145, 230, 300; Irving Harris, *The Breeze of the Spirit: Sam Shoemaker and the Story of Faith at Work* (New York: The Seabury Press, 1978), p. 10; Samuel M. Shoemaker, "How to Find God," reprint from *Faith at Work* Magazine, n.d., p. 6; *How You Can Help Other People* (New York: E. P. Dutton & Co., 1946), p. 60.

[37] Dick B., *Anne Smith's Journal*, pp. 20-22.

[38] Dick B., *That Amazing Grace*, p. 27.

[39] Samuel M. Shoemaker, Jr., *If I Be Lifted Up* (New York: Fleming H. Revell, 1931), p. 83; Glenn Clark, *Touchdowns for the Lord: The Story of "Dad" A. J. Elliott* (Minnesota: Macalester Park Publishing Company, 1947), pp. 55-56.

revelation (or guidance) from God.[40] 1 Corinthians 14:9-12, 14 state:

> But as it is written, Eye hath not seen, nor ear heard, neither have entered into the heart of man, the things which God hath prepared for them that love him. But God hath revealed *them* unto us by his Spirit: . . . even so the things of God knoweth no man, but the Spirit of God. Now we have received, . . . the spirit which is of God; that we might know the things that are freely given to us of God. . . . But the natural man receiveth not the things of the Spirit of God: for they are foolishness unto him: neither can he know *them*, because they are spiritually discerned.[41]

In the Old Testament and in the Gospels, God was able to communicate with people who had the spirit *upon* them:

> And I will come down and talk with thee [Moses] there: and I will take of the spirit which *is* upon thee, and will put *it* upon them. . . . And the Lord came down in a cloud, and spake unto him, and took of the spirit that *was* upon him, and gave *it* unto the seventy elders: and it came to pass, *that*, when the spirit rested upon them, they prophesied, and did not cease (Numbers 11:17, 25).

---

[40] The term "guidance"—much used by the Oxford Group to describe information received from the true God—doesn't occur in the King James Version of the Bible. However, the term "guide" does occur several times in such verses as: (1) Psalm 73:24: "Thou shalt guide me with thy counsel . . ."; and (2) Isaiah 58:11: "And the Lord shall guide thee . . ." "Revelation" is the biblical term for the Oxford Group concept of guidance. See, for example, Galatians 2:2 and Ephesians 3:3. There are three revelation manifestations of the gift of holy spirit, and these are mentioned in 1 Corinthians 12:7-11. They are: (1) word of knowledge, (2) word of wisdom, and (3) discerning of spirits.

[41] The word "natural" in verse 14 is translated from the Greek word *psuchikos*. In Jude 19, this Greek word is translated "sensual" in the King James Version and is accompanied by the appositive phrase, "having not the spirit." Not surprisingly, therefore, the NIV translates the first phrase in 1 Corinthians 2:14: "the man without the spirit." Romans 8:9 also sheds light on this topic: ". . . Now if any man have not the Spirit of Christ, he is none of his."

The Book of Isaiah adds this:

> As for me, this *is* my covenant with them, saith the Lord; my
> spirit that *is* upon thee, and my words which I have put in thy
> mouth, shall not depart out of thy mouth, nor out of the mouth
> of thy seed's seed, saith the Lord, from henceforth and forever
> (Isaiah 59:21).[42]

After Pentecost, it became possible for believers to receive the
gift of holy spirit *in* them and hence themselves to receive and
bring forth communications from God.[43] The following verses
illustrate what was promised and what believers received:

> And, behold, I [Jesus Christ] send the promise of my Father
> upon you; but tarry ye in the city of Jerusalem, until ye be
> endued with power from on high (Luke 24:49).[44]

> And, [he, Jesus Christ] being assembled together with *them* [the
> apostles], commanded them that they should not depart from
> Jerusalem, but wait for the promise of the Father, which, *saith*
> he, ye have heard of me. For John truly baptized with water; but
> ye shall be baptized with the Holy Ghost not many days hence.
> . . . ye shall receive power, after that the Holy Ghost is come
> upon you: and ye shall be witnesses unto me both in Jerusalem,
> and in all Judaea, and in Samaria, and unto the uttermost part of
> the earth (Acts 1:4-5, 8).[45]

> Then Peter said unto them, Repent, and be baptized every one of
> you in the name of Jesus Christ for the remission of sins, and ye
> shall receive the gift of the Holy Ghost. For the promise is unto

---

[42] See Streeter, *The God Who Speaks*, p. 114.

[43] See Streeter, *The God Who Speaks*, p. 109.

[44] See Streeter, *The God Who Speaks*, p. 125.

[45] See Streeter, *The God Who Speaks*, p. 111. See also Shoemaker's discussion in
Samuel M. Shoemaker, *With the Holy Spirit and with Fire* (New York: Harper and
Brothers, 1960), pp. 25-26.

you, and to your children, and to all that are afar off, *even* as many as the Lord our God shall call (Acts 2:38-39).

While Peter yet spake these words, the Holy Ghost fell on all them which heard the word. And they of the circumcision which believed were astonished, as many as came with Peter, because that on the Gentiles also was poured out the gift of the Holy Ghost. For they heard them speak with tongues, and magnify God (Acts 10:43-44).

But I [Paul] certify you, brethren, that the gospel which was preached of me is not after man. For I neither received it of man, neither was I taught *it*, but by revelation of Jesus Christ (Galatians 1:11-12).[46]

But when the fullness of time was come, God sent forth his Son, made of a woman, made under the law, to redeem them that were under the law, that we might receive the adoption of sons. And because ye are sons, God hath sent forth the Spirit of his Son into your hearts, crying Abba, Father. Wherefore thou art no more a servant, but a son; and if a son, then an heir of God through Christ (Galatians 4:4-7).[47]

Whereof I [Paul] am made a minister, according to the dispensation of God which is given to me for you, to fulfill the word of God; *Even* the mystery which hath been hid from ages and from generations, but now is made manifest to his saints: To whom God would make known what *is* the riches of the glory of this mystery among the Gentiles; which is Christ *in* you, the hope of glory (Colossians 1:25-27; italics added).[48]

---

[46] See Streeter, *The God Who Speaks*, p. 91; Macmillan, *Seeking and Finding*, p. 140.

[47] See Streeter, *The God Who Speaks*, p. 94.

[48] See the explanation of Oxford Group commentator Leslie D. Weatherhead, *Discipleship* (London: Student Christian Movement Press, 1934), pp. 146-147.

Sam Shoemaker devoted an entire chapter of his title, *National Awakening*, to explaining the relevance of surrender (via the new birth) as a prerequisite to keeping alive—through Bible study, public worship, prayer, and *listening*—the life that has been received through Christ in the new birth.[49]

---

[49] Samuel M. Shoemaker, Jr., *National Awakening* (New York: Harper & Brothers, 1936), pp. 55-66.

5

Quiet Time Practices

By the time "prayer and meditation" had reached A.A. itself, A.A.'s spiritual sources had defined very specifically what "quiet time" involved. Today's Twelve Step meditation often involves a five or ten minute glimpse at some dated, one-page reflection. Usually, there is no Bible verse involved. Often there is a quote from some "Conference Approved" A.A. literature; and the quote is frequently accompanied by comments of a writer who makes no mention of God, the Bible, or prayer. One A.A. historian recently commented:

> There are not only many "meditation books" today; there are too many. Squibs for "daily meditation" are useful, for beginners. But perhaps some are being locked into beginnerhood—into spiritual infancy. . . . Meditation, like food, loses nutrients when it is canned.[1]

We would add that meditation *books* neither or nor were the heart of the "morning watch" or "quiet time" or "prayer and meditation." Certainly not as morning and daily time with God were originally practiced by pioneer AAs or their forbears. Sam

---

[1] From Ernest Kurtz's Foreword in *The Soul of Sponsorship*, by Robert Fitzgerald, S. J. (Center City, MN: Hazelden, 1995), p. xi.

Shoemaker acknowledged that help via the reading of books and the receiving of instruction was often needed in getting *started*; but he pointed out that more was involved. As one of the pamphlets we will be citing as examples for the specific quiet time practices, Shoemaker said:

> Donald Carruthers' pamphlet on *How to Find Reality in Your Morning Devotions* has helped hundreds in this early stage: I was with him in China in the days when he was working out this pamphlet in the laboratory of experience, and I know it is born of experiment and not theory. There will be a constant tendency to drop back from the full faith that God's Holy Spirit can guide, and to say that the Bible is enough, or prayer is enough. . . . A full-orbed Quiet Time means Bible study, prayer, ample time to wait upon God in quiet, writing down what is given to us with those who are closest to us—certainly with husband or wife, or with one or more of the "spiritual family. . . ."[2]

Morning prayer time originally involved quality time devoted to practicing the presence of God. It involved substantial time. Quiet time. Peaceful time. Study of the Word of God. Sometimes with literary assistance in *that* study. Prayer. Listening. Writing down thoughts received. And checking with Scripture, often with other believers, to be sure that the thoughts received constituted genuine divine guidance and not just deception from some other spiritual source.

Before looking at what A.A. borrowed and where there is room for improvement in today's practices, we need to have before us a detailed picture of the precise practices that were developed by A.A.'s sources from the Bible, the Oxford Group, Sam Shoemaker's teachings, and the early Bible devotionals.

---

[2] Samuel M. Shoemaker, Jr., *The Conversion of the Church* (New York: Fleming H. Revell, 1932), p. 80.

A Definite, Adequate, Early Time

F. B. Meyer's question of Frank Buchman (which we covered earlier) did not really go to whether Buchman was "meditating" and receiving divine guidance. Essentially, the question was: "Do you give God *enough uninterrupted time* to tell you what to do?"

From that point on, Buchman and his First Century Christian Fellowship emphasized several things. They heeded the Biblical mandate that *morning* was the time to begin the walk with God.[3] They set aside half an hour to an hour in the morning for their meditation in the Bible, reading of helpful books, and two-way prayer (which involved speaking to God and listening to God). These practices took time. So did the writing down of thoughts to insure the thoughts were not forgotten and could be checked.

Time, then, was an important factor: a definite time, early time, morning time, fresh time, adequate time—adequate time to learn about God, to study about God's will, to petition God, and to hear from God. These "time" elements were the hallmark of the meditation which guided A.A.'s roots sources and produced early A.A.'s own prayer and meditation successes.

As a guide to the kind of time to be spent, Carruthers wrote:

Have a definite time each morning. The morning period before breakfast is most desirable. *Day telegrams* are delivered immediately. *Night letters* are delayed until the following morning. Give God the first moments of your day. It will remove the friction from the rest of the day's duties. The Psalmist wrote, "In the morning will I order my prayer unto thee, and will keep watch." It was a habit of Jesus, "a great while before it was day."[4]

---

[3] See discussion in Jack C. Winslow, *When I Awake* (London: Hodder & Stoughton, 1938), in the chapter titled "The Morning Watch," pp. 9-21.

[4] See Donald W. Carruthers, *How to Find Reality in Your Morning Devotions* (State College, PA., n.d.), p. 3. To compare the cited verses, see Psalm 5:3; Mark 1:35.

Sam Shoemaker clarified as to the "time" for Quiet Time, stating:

> Quiet Times do not need to be confined to morning and evening.
> One of the most profitable Quiet Times I have had was one
> Saturday afternoon on the top of a Fifth Avenue bus. The traffic
> swirled about us, but amid that confusion and noise God spoke
> to me as surely as ever He had at home or in the stillness of a
> church. I often stop in at Trinity Church, downtown, for a Quiet
> Time at noon, when things have gotten a bit on my nerves at the
> office. The early morning is the *best* time for Quiet, but not the
> *only* time.[5]

A Quiet, Peaceful, Relaxed Stance

"Time" was important in early meditation. But *so was the kind of
time*. The essence of "quiet" time, of course, was that the time
was to be "quiet."[6] Biblical instructions were: (a) "Be still, and
know that I am God. . . ." (Psalm 46:10).[7] (b) "Thou [God] wilt
keep *him* in perfect peace, *whose* mind *is* stayed *on thee*: because
he trusteth in thee" (Isaiah 26:3).[8] (c) ". . . Take no thought for
[don't be anxious about] your life, what ye shall eat, or what ye
shall drink; nor yet for your body, what ye shall put on. . . . for
your heavenly Father knoweth that ye have need of these things"
(Matthew 6:25, 32).[9] (d) "Be careful for [anxious about] nothing;
but in everything by prayer and supplication with thanksgiving let

---

[5] Samuel M. Shoemaker, Jr., *Children of the Second Birth* (New York: Fleming H. Revell, 1927), p. 97.

[6] See discussion in Winslow, *When I Awake*, in the chapter titled, "Entering Into Stillness," pp. 22-28.

[7] See Dick B., *The Good Book and The Big Book: A.A.'s Roots in the Bible* (San Rafael, CA: Paradise Research Publications, 1995), p. 156. This verse occurred often in the devotionals used by early AAs.

[8] See Dick B., *The Good Book and The Big Book*, p. 159. This verse also received much attention from the devotionals used by early AAs.

[9] See Dick B., *The Good Book and The Big Book*, p. 159. Dr. Bob firmly believed what he wrote in his personal story in the Big Book at page 181: "Your heavenly Father will never let you down!"

your requests be made known unto God. And the peace of God, which passeth all understanding, shall keep your hearts and minds through Christ Jesus" (Philippians 4:6-7).[10]

Shoemaker, and the others who taught AAs, *often* talked about "shutting the door." The morning time for Bible study, reading, prayer, listening, and checking was to be done and was done in an unhurried, relaxed, quiet, peaceful setting. Carruthers wrote:

> *Have a definite place where you can be alone.* Learn to concentrate on heavenly thoughts even surrounded by others amid real confusion. It is an art to become unmindful of others when absorbed in communion. Seek the out of doors frequently to feel the holy hush of nature newly born. Make your bedroom a gateway into His presence. Shut the door on the world and all that would distract. Closet yourself with the Lord Jesus. Let nothing on your part make such intimacy difficult.[11]

As mentioned above, the Bible itself called for being "still" (Psalm 46:10)—the better, we would add, to hear the "still small voice."[12] The Bible called for meditating, focusing thoughts, and "staying the mind" on God and His Word if one wanted the perfect peace necessary to receiving divine guidance.[13] The Bible also called for controlling one's mind—rejecting "anxiety."[14] Anxiety, a corollary of fear, simply defeated the believing necessary to receive God's help and guidance.

In his pamphlet, *How Can God Guide Me?*, Oxford Group writer Howard J. Rose suggested: "Get into a comfortable position—sit, recline or kneel, whichever gives greatest relaxation of mind and body. Cultivate stillness of mind by an act of will,

---

[10] See Dick B., *The Good Book and The Big Book*, p. 158, for the frequency with which this concept was quoted in A.A. devotional sources.

[11] Carruthers, *How to Find Reality in Your Morning Devotions*, p. 3.

[12] See 1 Kings 19:12.

[13] See, for example, Isaiah 26:3.

[14] See, for example, 2 Corinthians 10:5; Philippians 4:6-7.

thinking peaceful and restful thoughts. Have unhurried quiet and sense of leisure, avoiding all tenseness (Psalm 37:7)."[15]

Reading the Bible

Oxford Group people, and certainly Sam Shoemaker, agreed with Dr. Bob's wife Anne Smith that "the Bible ought to be the main Source Book of all. No day ought to pass without reading it."[16] Dr. Bob certainly followed this practice—daily.[17]

In his first title, Shoemaker wrote: "Read and know the Bible, and all else, including public worship, will fall in its place."[18] Since A.A.'s teachers spiritual regarded the Bible as the general or universal will of God, they hardly expected one to seek the will of God without studying and knowing the Word of God.

Shoemaker wrote:

> We find God's general will in the Scriptures. . . . [In] "Quiet Time". . . . Listening became the dominant note. Not the exclusive note: for there was Bible study first, taking a book and studying it straight through; and there was also ordinary prayer. . . . But the bulk of the time is listening. . . . And there are four next steps which they will need if they are to keep traveling. The first is their daily Quiet Time. At the beginning it will be simple, perhaps. They will need constant help, suggestions about how to study the Bible, where and what to read in it.[19]

---

[15] Howard J. Rose, *How Can God Guide Me?* (private pamphlet, n.d.: formerly *The Quiet Time*, published by the Oxford Group, n.d.), p. 2. Psalm 37:7 states: "Rest in the Lord, and wait patiently for him; fret not thyself because of him who prospereth in his way, because of the man who bringeth wicked devices to pass."

[16] See Dick B., *Anne Smith's Journal, 1933-1939: A.A.'s Principles of Success* (San Rafael, CA: Paradise Research Publications, 1995), p. 80.

[17] Dick B., *Dr. Bob's Library: Books for Twelve Step* Growth (San Rafael, CA: Paradise Research Publication, 1994), pp. 13-14.

[18] Samuel M. Shoemaker, Jr., *Realizing Religion* (New York: Association Press, 1923), p. 62.

[19] Shoemaker, *The Conversion of the Church*, pp. 49, 60, 79.

Now, guidance has got to become concrete and, in the best sense, habitual for ministers. This cannot come true without the setting apart of a definite time in the morning, the very first part of it, for sufficient prayer, Bible study, and listening for the Holy Spirit's directions.[20]

As we have previously shown, the Bible itself makes clear the vital necessity for *studying* Scripture: (a) "Study to shew thyself approved unto God. . . . rightly dividing the word of truth." (2 Timothy 2:15).[21] (b) "Search the scriptures. . . " (John 5:39).[22] And Acts commended believers in Berea, who received the word of God from Paul and Silas, but checked it out daily in Scripture itself. "These [the Bereans] were more noble than those in Thessalonica, in that they received the word with all readiness of mind, and searched the scriptures *daily*, whether those things were so" (Acts 17:11; italics added).

Oxford Group and Shoemaker adherents had catch word suggestions for Bible study: (1) Read it through. (2) Pray it in ["Ask God to open the Word to you and bring the Truth to light so that you might behold wondrous things"]. (3) Write it down ["Mark your Bible. Blaze the trail where the Light found you in your hour of need"]. (4) Work it out ["His words and His example and His influence still fling down their challenge upon us to "Be Christlike"] (5) Pass it On "[Avoid being afraid to share crusts of bread even when you have not yet been given the entire loaf. . . . 'Quickly, Go Tell'"].[23]

We will see in a moment why Oxford Group people checked their "luminous thoughts" (their "guidance") against Scripture to

---

[20] Samuel M. Shoemaker, Jr., *Twice-Born Ministers* (New York: Fleming H. Revell, 1929), p. 184.

[21] See Dick B., *The Good Book and The Big Book*, p. 157, for other references to this verse.

[22] See Dick B., *The Good Book and The Big Book*, p. 157.

[23] See Carruthers, *How to Find Reality in Your Morning Devotions*, pp. 1-3; Harry J. Almond, *Foundations for Faith*, 2d ed. (London: Grosvenor Books, 1980), pp. 30-31; Miles G. W. Phillimore, *Just for Today* (Privately published pamphlet, 1940), last page.

make sure what they heard was in fact divine guidance and conformed to the will of God as expressed in the word of God. To check one's thoughts against Scripture, one had to read, study, and know Scripture! Moreover, guidance from God enabled one, through the power of the holy spirit, to understand the universal will of God as communicated to mankind in the Bible. The two were interrelated.

Using Devotionals

In the author's opinion, the A.A. Step area that has gotten most out of whack, from an historical perspective, has to do with meditation books.[24] Some Twelve Step people today seem to look at meditation books as their sole daily spiritual diet. No Bible. No prayer. No listening. No assistance from clergy. Just reading what A.A. historian Ernest Kurtz called a "squib"—then dashing off into the maelstrom of life. But there is no evidence that this was the practice of the Oxford Group, of Sam Shoemaker, of those who regularly read the devotionals outside of A.A.'s environs, or even of the early AAs themselves.

A record from Acts 8 will illustrate the point. It concerns Philip, the revelation he received as to where to go to help a worshipper, and what was necessary for that searcher to know in order to understand the word of God. The chapter says, in part:

> And the angel of the Lord spake unto Philip, saying, Arise, and go toward the south unto the way that goeth down from Jerusalem unto Gaza, which is desert. And he arose and went: and, behold, a man of Ethiopia, an eunuch of great authority under Candace queen of the Ethiopians, who had the charge of all her treasure, and had come to Jerusalem for to worship, was returning, and sitting in his chariot read Esaias the prophet. Then the Spirit said unto Philip, Go near, and join thyself to this

---

[24] Big Book, p. 87, states: "There are many helpful books also. Suggestions about these may be obtained from one's priest, minister, or rabbi. Be quick to see where religious people are right. Make use of what they offer."

chariot. And Philip ran thither to *him*, and heard him read the prophet Esaias, and said, **Understandest thou what thou readest**? And he said, How can I, except some man should guide me? And he desired that he would come up and sit with him. The place of the scripture which he read was this, He was led as a sheep to the slaughter; and like a lamb dumb before his shearer, so opened he not his mouth; In his humiliation his judgment was taken away: and who shall declare his generation? for his life is taken from the earth. And the eunuch answered Philip, and said, I pray thee, of whom speaketh the prophet this? Of himself, or of some other man? Then Philip opened his mouth, and began at the same scripture, and preached unto him Jesus (Acts 8:26-35—bold print added).[25]

Two observations are important. Often, when he or she reads it, the student of the word of God simply cannot understand it when such person reads it without instruction or help.[26] Also, there are those—as in the foregoing case of Philip the evangelist—who have gift ministries to further the work of the church and aid students in understanding.[27] The suggestion in the Book of Acts is not that the eunuch did not need to read the Word, but rather that he needed some assistance in understanding it.

Devotionals and meditation books are *not* the word of God. At most, they are simply "helpful books." Sam Shoemaker wrote in his pamphlet *How to Find God*:

> *Read before you pray.* Read the Bible systematically. You may find *helpful* the serial books of devotion called Forward Day by Day, or the Upper Room or E. Stanley Jones' "Abundant Living." Use any devotional book that helps you. This draws

---

[25] See discussion in Samuel M. Shoemaker, *With the Holy Spirit and with Fire* (Harper and Brothers, 1960), pp. 32-33.

[26] Sometimes it is due to the fact that he or she does not have the spirit of God in them to enable them to discern spiritual truths. See 1 Corinthians 2:14.

[27] See Ephesians 4:11: "And he gave some, apostles; and some, prophets; and some, evangelists; and some, pastors and teachers."

your mind towards God, and makes you ready to pray (italics added).[28]

Concerning what one should do to help someone find Christ through surrender, Shoemaker was quoted as follows:

> They will need to form steady and adequate devotional habits. Prayer is a new experience. When shall they do it? How? With what help from books? Bible study must begin at once, but the most elementary instruction may be needed. A fine young churchman in my parish, who had started on a vital spiritual pilgrimage, said to me,"I have never read nor heard the Bible outside of church." That will go for tens of thousands of young people. Hand them a Bible, and they do not know where to turn. I suggested John 3, Romans 7 and 8, and Luke 12 and 15. But people need a plan—either a year-round lectionary, a plan to study a book at a time (which will require a commentary), or a topical study of, say, faith, or money, or prayer. We all ought to know, and have on hand, good books that help in this, books that initiate experience. I think a live church ought to have a book-stall, where vital books are on sale; and all of us ought to be good book salesmen, who make them known to others.[29]

Note that Shoemaker practiced what he preached. He maintained a book-stall at Calvary Church which contained, recommended through *The Calvary Evangel*, and distributed, all the important Oxford Group books of the 1930's.[30]

Note, however, that, in the Oxford Group, there was no substitute for the Word of God—an exacting study of it. Frank Buchman often said of the Bible: (1) Observe accurately. (2)

---

[28] Samuel M. Shoemaker, Jr., *How to Find God* (New York: Faith at Work, n.d.), p. 15.

[29] *Sam Shoemaker at His Best: Extraordinary Living for the Ordinary Man* (New York: Faith at Work, 1964), pp. 62-63.

[30] See Dick B., *Design for Living: The Oxford Group's Contribution to Early A.A* (San Rafael, CA: Paradise Research Publications, 1995), pp. 114-19.

Interpret honestly. (3) Apply drastically.[31] Devotionals were
simply used to *aid* the study.[32]

Praying *to* God

This will not be a discourse on prayer, for prayer was not the
expert province of Oxford Group people or of early AAs. Both had
some guidelines. And their root writings often did provide some
basic ideas about kinds of prayer and how to pray. The emphasis,
however, was on *listening*. Oxford Group people talked of "two-
way" prayer. Prayer was talking to God; but the dominant aspect
was listening.

Harry Emerson Fosdick was sometimes quoted by Oxford
Group writers; and Anne Smith recommended Fosdick's book on
The Meaning of Prayer.[33] In Fosdick's view, "Prayer is neither
chiefly begging for things, nor is it merely self-communing; it is
that loftiest experience within the reach of any soul, communion
with God."[34] Fosdick pointed to the comment of Brother
Lawrence about what praying meant to him (Brother Lawrence):
"That we should establish ourselves in a sense of God's presence,
by continually conversing with Him."[35]

There were, however, specific kinds of prayer A.A.'s root
sources mentioned. Anne Smith spoke of *intercessory prayer*
("pray that Spirit may tell you what to pray for").[36] She referred
to *petitionary prayers* ("Means expression of our wants which we

[31] Almond, *Foundations for Faith*, p. 31; Phillimore, *Just for Today*, last page.

[32] See, for example, K. D. Belden, *The Hour of the Helicopter* (Somerset, England: Linden Hall, 1992), pp. 21, 49; *Meeting Moral Re-Armament* (London: Grosvenor Books, 1979), p. 26.

[33] Dick B., *Anne Smith's Journal*, p. 82; Shoemaker, *Realizing Religion*, p. 64 (recommending Fosdick's book); Harry Emerson Fosdick, *The Meaning of Prayer* (New York: Association Press, 1915).

[34] Fosdick, *The Meaning of Prayer*, p. 32.

[35] Fosdick, *The Meaning of Prayer*, p. 33.

[36] Dick B., *Anne Smith's Journal*, p. 56; Jack C. Winslow, *When I Awake* (London: Hodder & Stoughton, 1938), p. 17; see Romans 8:26-27.

deeply feel and which it would be hypocrisy to pretend we didn't. These we submit . . . because He is our Friend. Similarly it would be unnatural not to submit to God the needs of others.").[37] Anne also discussed *prayers of praise—"adoration and thanksgiving."*[38] And Anne covered *prayers for guidance.* She herself cited Romans 2; but James 1:5 and Psalm 32:8 were two of the most commonly quoted verses (in A.A.'s root sources) which contained God's promises of guidance.[39]

Jack Winslow suggested several points about prayers in Morning Watch: (a) Opening moments of *silent adoration*: "Our spirit bows in humble and thankful adoration before our Creator."[40] (b) *Praise and thanksgiving*: "We praise God for all that He is in Himself. We thank Him for all that He has done, is doing, and will do."[41] (c) *The daily surrender*: "a simple act of will, by which we once again yield ourselves completely to the Divine Will, that God may direct and use us all the day through. This it is—since He will never force us—which makes us available to Him."[42] (d) *Intercession*: "My own usual practice is to restrict my early morning intercessions to *people* for whom I wish to pray, and it is a part of the morning watch that I would not on any

---

[37] Dick B., *Anne Smith's Journal*, p. 56; see Philippians 4:6-7; 1 John 5:14-15..

[38] Dick B., *Anne Smith's Journal*, p. 57; see 1 Thessalonians 5:18: "In every thing give thanks: for this is the will of God in Christ Jesus concerning you."

[39] James 1:5: "If any of you lack wisdom, let him ask of God, that giveth to all *men* liberally, and upbraideth not; and it shall be given him." Psalm 32:8: "I will instruct thee and teach thee in the way which thou shalt go: I will guide thee with mine eye." For the many A.A. sources quoting these verses, see Dick B., *The Good Book and The Big Book: A.A.'s Roots in the Bible* (San Rafael, CA: Paradise Research Publications, 1995), pp. 154-55.

[40] Winslow, *When I Awake*, pp. 28-29.

[41] Winslow, *When I Awake*, pp. 29-34.

[42] Winslow, *When I Awake*, pp. 35-40.

account let go."[43] (e) The *Prayer of Attention*: "Speak, Lord, for thy servant heareth."[44]

Shoemaker, of course, was a writing giant on the subject of prayer. But his focus was (and ours in this title is) on *listening*. In *The Conversion of the Church*, Shoemaker wrote, "Listening became the dominant note [in Quiet Time]. Not the exclusive note: for there [was] . . . 'also *ordinary prayer, confession*, petition, thanksgiving, intercession'" (italics added).[45]

Shoemaker also suggested the following:

> *Let great prayers help you to pray.* Make frequent use of books of prayer. Let us really know the treasure-houses of inspired devotional utterance. There comes a time in private prayer when we want to talk to God out of our hearts, and in our own words. But the prayers of others will help us to do this. As we fill those ancient and modern and universal prayers with our own needs, they will live for us, and help us to lift up our hearts to God.[46]

Hearing *from* God

In *Children of the Second Birth*, Shoemaker wrote:

> We believe entirely that conversion is the experience which initiates the new life. But we are not fools enough to think that the beginning is the end! All subsequent life is a development of the relationship with God which conversion opened. For us its daily focal point is what we call the "Quiet Time." As in all other private devotions, we pray and read the Bible. But the distinguishing element of a Quiet Time is listening for the

---

[43] Winslow, *When I Awake*, pp. 41-46; see James 5:15-16.

[44] Winslow, *When I Awake*, pp. 47-53; see 1 Samuel 3:9 and Dick B., *The Good Book and The Big Book*, p. 156, for a discussion of the many root sources quoting this verse.

[45] Shoemaker, *The Conversion of the Church*, p. 60.

[46] Samuel M. Shoemaker, Jr., *How to Find God* (New York: Faith at Work, n.d.), p. 16.

guidance of God. "Speak, Lord, for Thy servant heareth," is the expectant mood of a Quiet Time. The validity of what we believe to be God's guidance must show itself, in the long run, by more acute moral perception, more genuine human relationships, and increasing assurance of what one ought to do with each hour of the day.[47]

[Speaking of a Quiet Time with P.G.:] P.G. suggested a Quiet Time together. So they prayed together, opening their minds to as much of God as he understood, removing first the hindrance of self-will, allowing the Spirit to focus an impression upon the mind, like light upon a camera (p. 47).

Shoemaker always stressed the element of "letting go" to God and His Will. For example, he wrote:

There is a plan He has for us bigger than our own plan, and we are afraid of it. Somewhere we hold back. Somewhere we keep control of our own destiny. Let go! Abandon yourself to Him. Say to Him, "Not my will but Thine be done." Live it, Pray for it. Put yourself at His disposal for time and eternity.[48]

Several Oxford Group writers wrote some specifics about "listening." One specific involved the principle in a Chinese Proverb we have already mentioned: "God gave a man two ears and one mouth. Why don't you listen twice as much as you talk?"[49]

Cecil Rose wrote:

God has a plan. God speaks. But if He is to be heard and His plan is to be known and carried out, *man must listen.* That means a new approach to God for many of us. Our attitude when we

[47] Samuel M. Shoemaker, Jr., *Children of the Second Birth* (New York: Fleming H. Revell, 1927), p. 16.

[48] Shoemaker, *Religion That Works*, p. 19.

[49] Garth Lean, *Cast out Your Nets: Sharing Your Faith with Others* (London: Grosvenor, 1990), p. 25.

have prayed has been, "Listen, Lord, for Thy servant speaketh." Our prayer has been what Canon Streeter classifies as "pagan" prayer—the attempt to bend God to our desires and make Him the servant of our needs. . . . Prayer, when it consists of this one-sided address by us to God, becomes increasingly unreal and is eventually dropped or only formally retained. Christian prayer begins with the desire to know God's will for us. . . . The promise that our petitions will be answered is only to those who have first placed themselves in line with His Will. If God is to become for us the living, active God, at work directing our life and the world's, it is vital that we should learn how to listen. There is one condition to be fulfilled before we begin. We must be willing to hear anything God says to us. . . . The important thing is for us to make, each for himself, the thrilling discovery that God has spoken to us. Once we have made that discovery, God will shape our "quiet times" and develop them until they express a full personal relationship with Him, and include our thanksgiving, *worship*, petition, intercession, as part of our life with Him. . . . This does not mean that, when we have a "quiet time," we resign our reasoning powers. The idea that listening to God means making your mind a blank is a curious misconception which has hindered many people. It does mean that you leave room for God to lead you beyond your human thoughts, and tell you things you could never know yourself. The next thing we shall find is that we are able better to interpret God's other ways of speaking to us through circumstances, through other people, through the Bible. We are learning to know His voice in our "quiet time," and we recognize it better elsewhere (italics added).[50]

---

[50] Cecil Rose, *When Man Listens* (New York: Oxford University Press, 1937), pp. 30-34.

Addressing the question of how to begin, the Rev. Hallen Viney wrote:

"For one thing it means getting up earlier to listen to God. An alarm clock may be a help. If you feel chained to your bed, put the clock out of reach across the room." "How long should I listen?" "As long as you feel you need. Most of us began with a few minutes and find we need an hour or so now. Some people sit up in bed with a pencil and note-book, others dress first." "What happens? Do I hear a voice or something?" "No, God normally talks to people through their thoughts. It's the natural way for Him to reach you. Let Him put questions to you about your business, and your home life, and the bit of the world you live in. Think over the problems of the day against the background question, 'What does God want?' rather than 'What do I want?' You will find convictions forming in your mind as to the right thing to do. Write these convictions down."[51]

The Rev. Howard Rose had a host of specific comments about listening:

1. Get into a comfortable position, sit, recline or kneel, whichever gives greatest relaxation of mind and body. Cultivate stillness of mind by an act of will, thinking peaceful and restful thoughts. Have unhurried quiet and sense of leisure, avoiding all tenseness (Psalm 37:7).

2. Confess any known sin and seek forgiveness through Christ (1 John 1:5-9).

3. Seek the in-dwelling presence of Christ, claiming His promise "I am with you always." He is there. Realize Him. "Abide in me, and I in you." (Gal. 2:20).

4. Dedicate the body, soul and spirit to Him for the day. This act of committal entails the bringing to God the belief of the

---

[51] Hallen Viney, *How Do I Begin?* (New York: The Oxford Group, n.d.), p. 5.

mind, the love of the heart and the service of the will. (Rom. 12:1-2).

5. Pray that the Holy Spirit may take complete charge of the thought life, that only God's thoughts may enter the mind. (Romans 8:26-27; John 16:15).

6. In the attitude of "Speak Lord for Thy Servant heareth," wait patiently and quietly, listening for what He has to say, what He has to reveal to us concerning ourselves, what He wants us to do in His service, what message He wants us to hear, what piece of work He wants us to do, or what new truth He wants us to learn about Himself. (John 16:13-14).

Rose added: "Thoughts are given by way of: 1. Warnings: (a) Personal. (Wrong motives, thoughts, actions, etc., are revealed which might become an occasion for sin). (b) Concerning others. (Insight is given into the difficulties of those one is trying to help). 2. Some action to be taken, instructions re plans, etc. 3. Letters to write. 4. Visits to pay. 5. Thoughts to share with others. 6. Instructions re prayer, praise, what to read, etc. 7. Miscellaneous thoughts and promises."[52]

Oxford Group proponent Chaplain John E. Batterson wrote a simple pamphlet called *How to Listen to God*. In slightly more detail, Batterson covered the points Howard Rose covered. But he made some additional comments worth noting.

First, as to God, Batterson wrote:

1. God is alive. He always has been and He always will be. 2. God knows everything. 3. God can do anything. 4. God can be everywhere—all at the same time. (These three are the important differences between God and us human beings.). 5. God is invisible—we can't see Him or touch Him—But God is here. He is with you now. He is beside you. He surrounds you. He fills the room or the whole place where you are right now. He is in

---

[52] Howard J. Rose, *The Quiet Time*. Consult the entire four page pamphlet.

you now. He is in your heart. 6. God cares very much for you. He is interested in you. He has a plan for your life. He has an answer for every need and problem you face. 7. God will tell you all that you need to know. He will not always tell you all that you want to know. 8. God will help you do anything that He asks you to do. 9. Anyone can be in touch with God, anywhere and at any time, if the conditions are obeyed. These are the conditions: A. To be quiet and still. B. To listen. C. To be honest about every thought that comes. D. To test the thoughts to be sure that they come from God. E. To obey.[53]

Then, as to listening, Batterson said:

> TUNE IN. Open your heart to God. Either silently or aloud, just say to God in a natural way that you would like to find His plan for your life—you want His answer to the problem or situation that you are facing just now. Be definite and specific in your request (p. 2).

> LISTEN. Just be still, quiet, relaxed and open. Let your mind go "loose." Let God do the talking! Thoughts, ideas and impressions will begin to come into your mind and heart. Be alert and aware and open to every one (p. 2).

Writing Down Thoughts

From a number of different Oxford Group activists, the author has heard the story of how Oxford Group founder Dr. Frank Buchman explained the difference between "Guidance" and "Quiet Time." Buchman simply held up a pencil. The author recently sent one of his sponsees on a visit to a long-time Oxford Group "member" who knew Bill Wilson and actually went to meetings with Wilson. The Oxford Group adherent is now known to be the A.A. member with the greatest amount of sober time; for his sobriety began *before* Bill got sober, before Bill met Dr. Bob, and before Dr. Bob

---

[53] Chaplain John E. Batterson, *How To Listen to God* (pamphlet, n.d.), p. 1.

took his last drink—the latter time being the acknowledged founding date of A.A.[54] In any event, when the author's sponsee Bob met the Oxford Group survivor, Bob was encouraged to start observing Quiet Time, listen to God, and *write down thoughts.*
Explaining "Quiet Time," Sam Shoemaker wrote:

> Most of us find it indispensable to have a loose-leaf note-book, in which to write down the things which come to us. We find that in trying to remember what has come before, we block what is coming now: we find it impossible to remember sometimes the things which come even in a brief Quiet Time. The Chinese have a saying that "the strongest memory is weaker than the weakest ink." We do not want to forget the slightest thing that God tells us to do: and I have sometimes had a rush of detailed guidance which came almost as fast as I could write it.[55]

Shoemaker also said:

> *Fix the results of your praying by writing down what comes to you.* Many thoughts pass through your mind as you wait listening before God. Some are more important, some less; but writing them down will help you remember them, so that you can carry them out. Bishop Slattery, in some notes he made for an address, wrote, "Prayer—Note book—Wait—Listen—Write down what is given you." Take plenty of time for this, so as not to be hurried, or skimp your time with God. Twenty minutes at least every morning for *listening prayer.*[56]

---

[54] The Oxford Group person is Jim H. of Timonium, Maryland.

[55] Shoemaker, *The Conversion of the Church*, p. 60.

[56] Samuel M. Shoemaker, Jr., *How to Find God* (New York: Faith at Work, n.d.), p. 16.

Cecil Rose concurred with Shoemaker's view, stating:

> One practical hint is well worth taking. Use a note-book and
> pencil. Put down the thoughts which come in "quiet time." A
> typist who appeared minus her note-book when her employer
> wanted to dictate letters, would not hold her post long. It would
> not help her to plead that she could remember everything without
> taking it down. There is no reason why we should be less
> efficient with God. The Chinese say that the strongest memory
> is weaker than the palest ink.[57]

Howard Rose said:

> Many find it a real help to write down the ideas and thoughts
> which the Holy Spirit has caused to arise in the mind. The
> advantage of this is two-fold: it is an aid to concentration and
> acts as a reminder of duties to be performed. It is also of value
> in checking at the close of day the thoughts received each
> morning and through the day. (Jer. 30:2).[58]

"Checking" the Guidance

There has been criticism of the Oxford Group idea of
checking—criticism based either on lack of understanding of the
purpose of checking, belief that it is heretical, or criticism based
on the misapplication of the principle by Oxford Group people
themselves.[59] But the reason for "checking" is quite

---

[57] Cecil Rose, *When Man Listens* (New York: Oxford University Press, 1937), p. 37.

[58] Howard J. Rose, *How Can God Guide Me?* (formerly *The Quiet Time*) (London: privately published pamphlet, n.d.). p. 3. See also Viney, *How Do I Begin?*, pp. 3-4; Carruthers, *How to Find Reality in Your Morning Devotions*, pp. 9-10; Batterson, *How to Listen to God*, p. 2;

[59] Roman Catholic writer Dinger wrote: "Every Catholic knows that God does not, in His ordinary providence, give enlightenment of this kind in conducting the material aspects of life. Even the great mystics, who constantly lived under the influence of God, had to submit their inspiration to the independent control of the Church, ultimately, to

(continued...)

understandable; and—for Oxford Group people—essential if one is not to go awandering, telling himself and others that "God told me," when in fact the thoughts and guidance did not come from God.

Oxford Group adherents often quoted and relied upon James 1:17:

> Every good gift and every perfect gift is from above, and cometh down from the Father of lights, with whom is no variableness, neither shadow of turning.[60]

In other words, the true God will never steer us into trouble; hence *thoughts from God will be good thoughts.*

For Sinners Only laid out in detail the Oxford Group suggestions for making sure that "guidance" *was* guidance from God, and not from some other source. The tests as to the guidance received were:

1. Does it go counter to the highest standards of belief that we already possess?
2. Does it contradict the revelations which Christ has already made in or through the Bible?
3. Is it absolutely honest, pure, unselfish, loving?
4. Does it conflict with our real duties and responsibilities to others?
5. If still uncertain, wait and continue in prayer, and consult a trustworthy friend who believes in the guidance of the Holy Spirit.[61]

---

[59] (...continued)
insure divine authenticity." See Rev. Clair M. Dinger, S.T.L., *Moral Re-Armament: A Study of Its Technical and Religious Nature in the Light of Catholic Teaching* (Washington, D.C., The Catholic University of America Press, 1961), p. 59.

[60] See Dick B., *The Good Book and the Big Book*, pp. 40, 72, 89-90, 187; The Layman with a Notebook, *What is The Oxford Group?* (London: Oxford University Press, 1933), p. 67; C. Irving Benson, *The Eight Points of the Oxford Group* (London: Oxford University Press, 1936), p. 79.

[61] A. J. Russell, *For Sinners Only* (London: Hodder & Stoughton, 1932), p. 94.

Oxford Group people commonly pointed out they did not believe that every thought received in Quiet Time was a thought or directive from God. Therefore, they checked thoughts to be sure the thoughts accorded with God's will as expressed in the Bible, with the teachings of Jesus Christ, and with other Biblical principles of love. And the author has laid out in several other titles the principles of, objections to, and tests for, guidance as the Oxford Group saw the process.[62]

Cecil Rose wrote:

> Of course, every thought that comes to us in the "quiet time" is not God's guidance. We need to test the voices that come to us along a line that has been so long disused or blocked. We have immediate cause to reject promptings which conflict with what we already know of His will. Nothing which is unloving, impure, dishonest, or selfish comes from God. Other suggestions which come to us may have to be talked out with some experienced person who knows how to listen to God. In other cases we may have to wait for clearer conviction in our own minds. Sometimes the only test is to make the venture and act. We shall make mistakes. But an honest mistake is of far more use to God than the timid inaction which makes no venture.[63]

Note the following from the Book of James, a favorite with early AAs:

> But if ye have bitter envying and strife in your hearts, glory not, and lie not against the truth. This wisdom descendeth not from above, but *is* earthly, sensual, devilish. For where envying and strife *is*, there *is* confusion and every evil work. But the wisdom that is from above is first pure, then peaceable, gentle, *and* easy

---

[62] Dick B., *Design for Living*, pp. 260-69. See also Forde, *The Guidance of God*, pp. 19-22.

[63] Rose, *When Man Listens*, p. 35.

to be intreated, full of mercy and good fruits, without partiality, and without hypocrisy (James 3:14-17).[64]

Small wonder there was vital necessity for checking which wisdom was from which source!

Clearing the Receiver

It is beyond the scope of this title to discuss at any length the Oxford Group concepts of "Sin," the "Five C's," and the "Four Absolutes."[65] But the Oxford Group *was* about life-changing through the power of Jesus Christ. And the foregoing three groups of ideas were critical to the life-changing process. Sin, said the Oxford Group, was anything that blocked you from God and from other people. The Five C's were the principal elements in the life-changing program of "soul surgery" that cut the blocks of sin away through the power of God and enabled the adherent to have an experience of Christ and change his or her life. The tests for the "sins" or shortcomings that needed to be removed were the four "standards" or four "absolutes" as they were variously called—absolute honesty, absolute purity, absolute unselfishness, and absolute love. These four standards were the marks of the perfect life Jesus Christ lived and taught. They were the "yardsticks" (as Dr. Bob called them) or goals by which Oxford Group people tried to measure their lives and toward which they pointed their actions. These Oxford Group people were seeking to "put off the old man" and "to put on the new man" which they had received by reason of their rebirth and changed lives.[66]

---

[64] For Oxford Group references to this verse, see Dick B., *Design for Living*, pp. 232, 242.

[65] For full discussion, see Dick B., *The Oxford Group & Alcoholics Anonymous*, pp. 29-33, 103-04, 166-70, 175-81, 184-211, 221-69.

[66] See Ephesians 4:22, 24. See how Clarence S. quoted these verses in connection with the Third Step of Alcoholics Anonymous. Dick B., *That Amazing Grace: The Role of Clarence and Grace S. in Alcoholics Anonymous* (San Rafael, CA: Paradise Research Publications, 1996), p. 68.

For us, it is important to know that they believed the "lens" had to be clear for the reborn people to receive messages from God. The "receiving set" had to be in good order. Even Bill's wife, Lois Wilson, touched on some of the points in the following extracts from notations in her "Oxford Group Notebook":

1. "Definite adequate, accurate information from God."

3. "Sat. A.M. Chas Haines—Bible . . . Home Quiet Time."
4. "I realized that I had not really put my reliance in God but have been trying under guidance as I thought to do it all myself."

6. "List of sins: Feeling of being special, self conscious, feeling of inferiority, self-indulgence in small things, dependency on human law."
7. "Sin blinds, binds, multiplies, deadens."

9. "Oxford Group is spiritual revolution whose concern is vital Christianity under dictatorship of spirit of God."
10. "A new spirit is abroad in the world, a new illumination can bring men & women of every social situation back to the basic principles of the Christian faith."

14. "Helen Shoemaker—Surrender to God."

In these limited remarks, Lois was expressing what she had heard and noted about the removal of "blocks to God" at the Oxford Group meetings and houseparties she and Bill had attended.[67] The Oxford Group was concerned with removing the blocks (blocks in the form of sin that "blinds, binds, multiplies, and deadens") that prevented an effective relationship with God and prevented receiving guidance from God.[68] Simple expressions of

---

[67] See Dick B., *The Akron Genesis of Alcoholics Anonymous*, pp. 150-55.
[68] See Dick B., *Design for Living*, pp. 192-97.

the need for getting the receiving set in order can be found in the following Oxford Group statements:

> Remember, there are one or two conditions attached to this listening. It's rather like telephoning; God can't talk through a dirty contact. If you want to hear what He has to say, you must first find out, as I had to, whether you've got a good connection. . . . if you really want to listen to God you have to be more definite. If something goes wrong with the telephone, the trouble shooter doesn't say, "I don't claim this telephone is working well, but it's as good as the next one. First of all he's got to find the fault in the telephone and then put it right. . . . there are four pretty good tests to help you to be definite in finding these faults. They are absolute honesty, absolute purity, absolute unselfishness, and absolute love. When I first met this Oxford Group crowd I didn't know much about religion, but I did know what honesty meant, and when I thought about absolute honesty some very concrete faults came into my mind. It was uncomfortably definite. . . . Well, like the trouble shooter with the faulty telephone, it's not enough just to know what is wrong and leave it at that. The thing is to put it right . . . . Don't worry about the theory now. A lot of people can switch on the light without knowing much about electricity. The main thing is to get the light. In the same way, a lot of people get into first-hand touch with God without knowing all the theory at first.[69]

The Oxford Group life-changing principles of decision, moral inventory, confession, conviction, conversion, restitution, and continuance spilled over into A.A.'s Twelve Steps. In fact, the steps are framed on those ideas. And critically important to A.A.'s prayer and meditation Step was the elimination of spiritual infirmities by which "we [the AAs] shut ourselves off from sunlight of the Spirit."[70] It was about cleaning the lens. Clearing

---

[69] Viney, *How Do I Begin?*, pp. 2-4.

[70] *Alcoholics Anonymous*, 3rd ed. (New York City: Alcoholics Anonymous World Services, 1976), p. 66.

the receiving set. The author (Dick B.) would call it getting back into fellowship with God (See 1 John, Chapter One).

Chaplain Batterson wrote about "blocks" to receiving guidance, saying:

> BLOCKS? What if I don't seem to get any definite thoughts? God's guidance is as freely available as the air we breathe. If I am not receiving thoughts when I listen, the fault is not God's. Usually it is because of something *I will not do*: A. Something wrong in my life that I will not face and make right. B. A habit or indulgence I will not give up. C. A person I will not forgive. D. A wrong relationship in my life I will not give up. E. A restitution I will not make. F. Something God has already told me to do that I will not obey. Check these points and be honest. Then try listening again.[71]

Obeying the "Voice"

As the author of *For Sinners Only* said, John 7:17 was often considered Sam Shoemaker's favorite verse.[72] For the Oxford Group people, the verse had to do with *obedience*. Shoemaker quoted John 7:17 and said:

> A moral experiment is worth ten times an intellectual investigation in apprehending spiritual truth. Obedience is as much the organ of spiritual understanding as reason. Many people have come into a personal and living faith by trying the experiment which is implied in: "If any man willeth to do his will, he shall know."[73]

---

[71] Batterson, *How to Listen to God*, p. 3. See similar language in Shoemaker, *Twice-Born Ministers*, p. 92.

[72] Russell, *For Sinners Only*, p. 211; see John 7:17: "If any man will do his will, he shall know of the doctrine, whether it be of God, or *whether* I speak of myself."

[73] Shoemaker, *Religion That Works*, p. 36.

Again, it is beyond the purview of this title to discuss the tremendous significance of the Oxford Group's "experiment of faith" based on John 7:17. But A.A.'s own "program of action" and the Oxford Group's program for change were based on the idea that one could hear from God and receive the benefits of God's guidance when one *obeyed* God's known directives, whether they were set out in the Bible itself or received through messages from God. The key to listening was starting the experiment by making a decision, finding and forsaking the faults, righting the wrongs, and then tuning in to God.

As we've said, Frank Buchman was famous for the statement:

> God alone can change human nature. The secret lies in that great forgotten truth that when man listens, God speaks; when man obeys, God acts.[74]

What Oxford Group Pioneers Report Today

Recently, the author circulated a questionnaire among Oxford Group survivors who were alive and active in the O.G. fellowship and teams in the 1930's when A.A.'s own spiritual recovery ideas were being formulated. Some of these pioneers actually met A.A. co-founder Bill Wilson and went to Oxford Group meetings with him, though they did not necessarily remember him well.[75]

---

[74] Buchman, *Remaking the World*, p. 46.

[75] Those who had responded at the date of this writing were: Sydney Cook of Heath Cardiff, England; Michael B. Hutchinson of Oxford, England; the Reverend Harry J. Almond of North Egremont, Massachusetts; Terence Blair of Richmond, Virginia (now, deceased, and whose wife replied); Dr. Richard Hadden of St. Ignace, Michigan; James Houck of Timonium, Maryland; the Reverend T. Willard Hunter of Claremont, California; James Draper and Eleanor Forde Newton of Fort Myers Beach, Florida; L. Parks Shipley, Sr., of Hightstown, New Jersey; and George Vondermuhll, Jr. of Bloomfield, Connecticut. Previously, the author had received information from Kenneth D. Belden, Garth Lean (deceased), and Dr. Robin C. Mowat of the United Kingdom. James Houck knew, and went to Oxford Group meetings attended by, Bill Wilson and the Rev. Sam Shoemaker in Maryland. Eleanor Forde Newton was quoted in Anne

(continued...)

The purpose of the survey was to see: 1) What the Oxford Group people remembered about the practices they followed in Quiet Time; 2) The Bible verses they remembered in connection with Guidance, Quiet Time, Bible study, Prayer, and Listening; and 3) The devotionals and other literature they used as guides. The assumption was and is that if these were the things Oxford Group people remember doing, we could reasonably assume that Bill and Lois Wilson, Dr. Bob and Anne Smith, Henrietta Seiberling, T. Henry and Clarace Williams, Clarence S., and the other A.A. pioneers were doing these things also; for all these "founders" of A.A. were very much involved in the Oxford Group at the beginnings of A.A. As Bill Wilson once put it: "In Akron, they [the local A.A. members] were the Oxford Group, or at least many thought they were, until the book [*Alcoholics Anonymous*] came out in 1939."[76] Bill only stated the half of it. Actually, early AAs in Akron usually *called themselves* "the alcoholic squad of the Oxford Group" or a "Christian Fellowship," after the Oxford Group's other name, "A First Century Christian Fellowship."[77]

George Vondermuhll, Jr., former corporate secretary for Moral Re-Armament in America, pointed out several facts. First, that the Oxford Group was not an "organization." Second, that there was no "handbook, list of prescribed or suggested 'guide books' for QT or Daily Meditation, etc." Third, that "Different individuals and groups in different, or even the same, places used one or several or many of the above [the guide books, Bible verses, and devotionals listed in the questionnaires] at times."

---

[75] (...continued)
Smith's Journal. James D. Newton was recorded in Lois Wilson's Oxford Group Notebook as having met Lois and Bill Wilson. And Parks Shipley knew, and attended Oxford Group meetings with, Bill Wilson at Calvary House in New York.

[76] *DR. BOB and the Good Oldtimers* (New York: Alcoholics Anonymous World Services, Inc., 1980), p. 155. See also p. 137.

[77] *DR. BOB*, pp. 53-54, 117-18, 128, 156.

Principal Guide Books Used:

Almost every respondent confirmed his or her use of the following: *The Guidance of God* by Eleanor Napier Forde (Newton), *When Man Listens* by Cecil Rose, *The Quiet Time* by Howard Rose, *The God Who Speaks* by Burnett Hillman Streeter, and *How Do I Begin?* by Hallen Viney.

A couple of the Oxford Group survivors confirmed using as a "textbook" *What Is The Oxford Group?* by The Layman with a Notebook. A couple mentioned Jack C. Winslow's books, particularly *When I Awake*. One referred to *How to Find Reality in Your Morning Devotions* by Donald W. Carruthers. One suggested adding *The Greatest Thing in the World* by Henry Drummond. And one commented: "We drew on the first-person experiences chronicled in *For Sinners Only* [by A. J. Russell], *Life Began Yesterday* [by Stephen Foot], and later on Buchman's collected speeches in *Remaking the World*."

In assembling the bibliographies for his various titles, the author also relied on the recommended list of Oxford Group Literature which the Reverend Sam Shoemaker included in his parish publication *The Calvary Evangel* during the 1930 period. Also, the author consulted the back cover of some of the Oxford Group publications from Great Britain during the 1930's; for these also listed recommended Oxford Group literature.

Daily Meditation Books in Quiet Time:

One should realize that most of the daily meditation books used in the 1930's were similar in format. There was a page for each day. It would therefore be unusual to find an Oxford Group person consulting several meditation books for any given day. Hence the books that were mentioned by a pioneer tended to represent his or her own choice as to the particular devotional that person utilized.

Highest on the list of choices was *My Utmost for His Highest* by Oswald Chambers. Mrs. W. Irving Harris, widow of Sam Shoemaker's assistant minister, once told the author (during a

conversation several years ago) about the wide use of the
Chambers devotional in the Oxford Group. But she said Chambers
was not connected with the Oxford Group fellowship. Oxford
Group historian Mark O. Guldseth wrote: "Oswald Chambers was
a Scotsman who was influenced in his early years by Charles
Spurgeon, F. B. Meyer, and Jessie Penn-Lewis. One of his books,
My Utmost for His Highest, was widely read by Buchman's early
associates."[78]

Other respondents mentioned Harry Emerson Fosdick's *The
Meaning of Prayer*, *Victorious Living* by E. Stanley Jones, *Daily
Strength for Daily Needs* by Mary W. Tileston; and one mentioned
The Upper Room. Michael Hutchinson from Oxford and Jim
Houck from Maryland both pointed out that many people have
used *A New Day* by Dorothy M. Prescott. This book was not
published until 1957 but did contain many references to earlier
Oxford Group writings and ideas.

All the foregoing meditation books (except *A New Day*) were
used by Dr. Bob and Anne Smith. Bill Wilson must have read *The
Upper Room* which was in such wide use in early Akron A.A. And
Bill and Lois Wilson definitely studied *My Utmost for His Highest*
quite often.

Bible Verses Accepted As Relevant to Quiet Time:

Most of the Oxford Group pioneers acknowledged that the
following verses were relevant to the Quiet Time ideas of Bible
study, prayer, listening, and writing down notes: (1) Jeremiah
30:2: "Write thee all the words that I have spoken unto thee in a
book." (2) Psalm 46:10: "Be still, and know that I am God." (3)
1 Samuel 3:9: "Speak, Lord; for thy servant heareth." (4) James
1:5: "If any of you lack wisdom, let him ask of God, that giveth
to all *men* liberally, and upbraideth not; and it shall be given him."
Some confirmed the relevance of Psalm 5:3: "My voice shalt thou

[78] Mark O. Guldseth, *Streams* (Fritz Creek, Alaska: Fritz Creek Studios, 1983), p. 160.

hear in the morning, O Lord; in the morning will I direct *my prayer* unto thee, and will look up;" and Isaiah 26:3: "Thou wilt keep *him* in perfect peace, *whose* mind *is* stayed *on thee*: because he trusteth in thee."

Bible Verses Concerning Revelation:

Though some expressed familiarity with Galatians 1:12; 2 Timothy 3:16; 1 Corinthians 12:8; and 2 Peter 1:21, almost every respondent confirmed the relevance to him or her of John 14:26: "But the Comforter, *which is* the Holy Ghost, whom the Father will send in my name, he shall teach you all things, and bring all things to your remembrance, whatsoever I have said unto you."

Bible Verses Concerning Revelation to the Individual:

There was almost uniform agreement that the following verses confirmed that God could and would speak to the individual: (1) Psalm 32:8: "I will instruct thee and teach thee in the way which thou shalt go: I will guide thee with mine eye." (2) Psalm 37:5: "Commit thy way unto the Lord; trust also in him; and he shall bring *it* to pass. (3) Proverbs 3:6: "In all thy ways acknowledge him, and he shall direct thy paths." (4) Acts 9:6: "Lord, what wilt thou have me to do?" (5) Acts 22:10: "What shall I do, Lord?" (6) Romans 8:14: "For as many as are led by the Spirit of God, they are the sons of God." (7) 2 Corinthians 5:7: "For we walk by faith, not by sight."

Some Important Verses Added through the Survey:

Michael Hutchinson called attention to the importance in the Oxford Group of the following additional relevant verses: (1) 1 Kings 19:12: ". . . a still small voice" [speaking of the voice of the Lord]. (2) Isaiah 50:4: ". . . he wakeneth morning by morning. he wakeneth mine ear to hear as the learned." (3) Jeremiah 7:23: "Obey my voice, and I will be your God, and ye shall be my people: and walk ye in all the ways that I have commanded you, that it may be well with you." (4) Amos 8:11: "Behold, the days come, saith the Lord God, that I will send a famine in the land, not a famine of bread, nor a thirst for water, but of hearing the words of the Lord." (5) John 6:45: "It is written in the prophets, and they shall be all taught of God. Every man therefore that hath heard, and hath learned of the Father, cometh unto me."

A Look at Three of the Devotionals

As stated, Oswald Chambers' *My Utmost for His Highest* was widely used as an "helpful book" by Oxford Group people in connection with their morning devotions. This meditation book is still widely sold and available. And to give the reader an idea of what the book contains, we will quote from page 317. This page covers November 12th. It is titled "The Transfigured Life." It deals with 2 Corinthians 5:17—the verse which A.A.'s Clarence S. states was responsible for changing his life, and a verse which was widely mentioned in early A.A.

In his book, Chambers quotes the verse and then states:

What idea have you of the salvation of your soul? The experience of salvation means that in your actual life things are really altered, you no longer look at things as you used to; your desires are new, old things have lost their power. One of the touchstones of experience is—Has God altered the thing that matters? If you still hanker after the old things, it is absurd to talk about being born from above, you are juggling with yourself. If you are born again, the Spirit of God makes the alteration manifest in your actual life and reasoning, and when the crisis comes you are the most amazed person on earth at the wonderful difference there is in you. There is no possibility of imagining that *you* did it. It is this complete and amazing alteration that is the evidence that you are a saved soul. What difference has my salvation and sanctification made? For instance, can I stand in the light of 1 Corinthians xiii, or do I have to shuffle? The salvation that is worked out in me by the Holy Ghost emancipates me entirely, and as long as I walk in the light as God is in the light, He sees nothing to censure because His life is working out in every particular, not by my consciousness, but deeper than my consciousness.

Mary Wilder Tileston's *Daily Strength for Daily Needs* covers Matthew 6:28 on page 169 for June 17th. The title of the page is "Consider the lilies of the field, how they grow." There is a poem which concludes "in their loveliness appear, and grow, and smile and do their best, and unto God they leave the rest." The first paragraph suggests: "Interpose no barrier to His mighty life-giving power, working in you all the good pleasure of His will. . . . Put your growing into His hands as completely as you have put all your other affairs. Suffer Him to manage as He will. Do not concern yourself about it, nor even think of it. Trust Him absolutely and always. . . . Say a continual 'yes' to your Father's will." The second paragraph suggests: "Thine own self-will and anxiety, thy hurry and labor, disturb thy peace, and prevent Me from working in thee. Look at the little flowers, in the serene summer days; they quietly open their petals, and the sun shines into them with his gentle influences. So will I do for thee, if thou wilt yield thyself to Me."

The Upper Room began publishing its quarterlies at the time A.A. was founded. Its page for June 9th, the day before Dr. Bob took his last drink, deals with Acts 1:8, the day of Pentecost, and the receipt of the power of the holy spirit. First, the page quotes Acts 1:8: "Ye shall receive power after that the Holy Ghost is come upon you." Next, the page tells a little story of a stranded fisherman who worked with his neighbors to extricate his boat from the mud. The power of the tide, says the story, lifted the vessel out of the mud and set her afloat again. The paragraphs conclude with these statements: "Nevertheless, the truth remains that we cannot by our own strength save ourselves or the world. When the Spirit of God sweeps upon us, like the tide of the sea, we shall be lifted out of the mud and we shall have power over the hearts of men." The reader is then urged, "Read Acts 2:1-13."

This is, of course, the account of the birth of the Christian Church on Pentecost when the Apostles received the power of the holy spirit and manifested the power by speaking in tongues. The page contains a prayer: "O Lord, revive Thy Church—and begin with me. Amen." The "Thought for the Day" was this: "The first duty of every Church and every Christian is to tarry at Jerusalem (Acts 1:4). We cannot do the work of God until we have received the power of God. And every day we should tarry until we are conscious of the Spirit's renewed glow and power."

6

What Early AAs Borrowed

To readers looking for help in practicing the Twelve Steps, it may have seemed unnecessary to review how Quiet Time was observed before and as of the time A.A.'s own guidance ideas were being formulated. But, at countless A.A. meetings, the author has heard so many bewildered and half-baked statements about meditation that it seemed vitally important to set forth above precisely *why and how* A.A.'s progenitors observed Quiet Time.

Let's consider some examples (from the author's own experience) which illustrate the need for understanding where A.A.'s meditation ideas came from.

The first concerns an A.A. oldtimer, who regularly attended a "Step Study" meeting frequented by the author. This AA often evoked titters from the meetings when he would almost invariably say he used to think wrongly that the Eleventh Step meant he would hear a whispered voice saying: "Invest here." Then the man would say the Eleventh Step was not his "long suit," but he shared little information on what it *did* mean to him. Later, the author was to learn that the man had never read the Bible and had some vague idea (probably derived from the writings of Emmet Fox)—a book many AAs read today—that *everyone* has "Christ" in him.[1]

---

[1] Compare Romans 10:9; Ephesians 2:1-22; 3:1-17; Colossians 1:23-28.

Next, there was one of the author's A.A. friends—a devout Christian and also a physician— who was relating to the author a story about his early sobriety. The doctor was on a trip with his wife, got in a snit, and jumped angrily from the car crying: "Intuit me, intuit me." He expressed great frustration over receiving no message as to how to handle the problem. The man *did* believe in the guidance of God. At that point in his early sobriety, however, he had little appreciation of some of the vital principles involved in receiving guidance—peace and lack of anxiety, for openers.[2]

Finally, the author recently found himself talking at an A.A. meeting with a learned professor who was discussing the subject of "guidance." The man said he believed in guidance, but not the "parking place" variety. The educator said he thought it absurd that some people believed God could direct them to a much needed and sought after parking place. Assuming some things about the man's religious and believing background, the author remained silent. But he found it difficult not to ask the man what he thought of Paul's statement in Philippians 4:19: "But my God shall supply your need according to his riches in glory by Christ Jesus." Or, about Dr. Bob's statement at the end of his personal story in the Big Book: "Your Heavenly Father will never let you down!" (p. 181).

There are, of course, countless other examples in the author's own experience of A.A.-self constructed religious ideas which certainly do not come from A.A.'s roots and find little or no support in the language of the Twelve Steps or A.A.'s basic text, *Alcoholics Anonymous*. The author has heard several who have just been arrested for driving without a license or without insurance come, at one time or another, to meetings proclaiming that God was trying to teach them something through their arrest.[3] Others have said they just had to "accept" some major, frightening calamity or disaster, scarcely or never mentioning what trusting in

---

[2] Compare Matthew 6:25-33; Philippians 4:6-7; Isaiah 26:3-4.
[3] Compare James 1:12-17; 2:14-18.

God for guidance or deliverance really means.[4] Still others assign blame to themselves and reek of self-condemnation at every bad turn in life, talking of being content with the cards that are dealt to them, seemingly blind to the fact that there is not only another source of life's difficulties, but also another source for victory over them.[5]

With that, we can turn to what early A.A. really did abstract from its rich, spiritual roots in the realm of prayer and meditation. And we will do so primarily by looking at the Third Edition of A.A.'s basic text, *Alcoholics Anonymous*—which AAs affectionately call their "Big Book."[6]

The Text of the Eleventh Step

Let's begin with the precise wording of Step Eleven itself: "Sought through prayer and meditation to improve our conscious contact with God *as we understood Him*, praying only for knowledge of His Will for us and the power to carry that out." As we've stated, Bill Wilson said specifically that the ideas for prayer and meditation came from the Oxford Group.

First, let's look at "contact with God." Though not necessarily unique to the Oxford Group, the language was Oxford Group language.[7] Second, at "conscious contact" with God or, as Oxford

---

[4] Compare Proverbs 3:5-6.

[5] Compare John 10:10; Romans 8:35-39; 1 Corinthians 2:4-16; 2 Corinthians 3:4-6; 4:3-4.

[6] See also Dick B., *The Good Book and The Big Book* (San Rafael, CA: Paradise Research Publications, 1995).

[7] Sam Shoemaker's friend and Oxford Group colleague Dr. Philip Marshall Brown wrote "of the charity and love that are poured into human beings whenever they establish contact with God." See Philip Marshall Brown, *The Venture of Belief* (New York: Fleming H. Revell, 1935), p. 24. Oxford Group writer Stephen Foot said: "Contact with God is the necessary fundamental condition, and that is made through prayer and listening . . ." See Stephen Foot, *Life Began Yesterday* (London: William Heinemann, Ltd., 1935), p. 16.

Group people called it, "God consciousness."[8] Third, at the phrase "God as we understood Him." This concept of surrendering as much of ourselves as we understand to as much of God as we understand was Oxford Group all the way.[9]

And what of prayer for "knowledge of His will for us and the power to carry that out"? As shown previously the writings of Stephen Foot bring to mind this compellingly similar language used by Oxford Group adherent Foot: "I will ask God to show me His purpose for my life and claim from Him the power to carry that purpose out."[10]

There are other similarities between the Big Book language, and Oxford Group and Shoemaker writings. But the important thing here is that both the *language* of Step Eleven and the *idea* of praying for knowledge of God's will and for the power to carry out that will were Oxford Group in thinking. So was the idea of "prayer and meditation." It came from the Bible, as our Bible citations have shown.

A. J. Russell's popular book also showed the Oxford Group linkage between God's guidance and God's power:

> God had a plan. They were trying to fit in with it. Knowledge of that plan, God's guidance and God's power were available for all who chose to work in with that plan. This guidance and power transcended every form of self-determination. God-guidance in

---

[8] See Harold Begbie, *Life Changers*, 12th ed. (London: Mills & Boon, Ltd, 1932), p. 39; Victor C. Kitchen, *I Was a Pagan* (New York: Harper & Brothers, 1934), pp. 41, 43, 75; Samuel M. Shoemaker, Jr., *Twice-Born Ministers* (New York: Fleming H. Revell, 1929), p. 123.

[9] See Samuel M. Shoemaker, Jr., *Children of the Second Birth* (New York: Fleming H. Revell, 1927), pp. 47, 25; *How to Become a Christian* (New York: Harper & Brothers, 1953), p. 72; Dick B., *The Good Book and The Big Book*, pp. 53-62; *Design for Living: The Oxford Group's Contribution to Early A.A.* (San Rafael, CA: Paradise Research Publications, 1995), p. 306.

[10] Foot, *Life Began Yesterday*, p. 13.

God's strength could be the normal experience of everybody at all times.[11]

There was a well-known Oxford Group saying that "Where God guides, He provides." The listener had but to listen for the will of God, and the power to carry it out would be present for the taking.

Big Book Examples of Guidance Language

There is scarcely a part of the Big Book that does not involve requests for God's guidance and direction.[12] Following are several examples:

> I placed myself unreservedly under His care and direction (p. 13).

> I was to sit quietly when in doubt, asking only for direction and strength to meet my problems as He would have me (p. 13).

> They found that a new power, peace, happiness, and sense of direction flowed into them (p. 50).

> When we drew near to Him He disclosed Himself to us (p. 57)!

> God will show us how to take a kindly and tolerant view of each and every one (p. 67).

> We ask Him to remove our fear and direct our attention to what He would have us be (p. 68).

> In meditation, we ask God what we should do about each specific matter. The right answer will come, if we want it (p. 69).

---

[11] A. J. Russell, *For Sinners Only* (London: Hodder & Stoughton, Ltd., 1932), p. 23.

[12] See Dick B., *New Light on Alcoholism: The A.A. Legacy from Sam Shoemaker* (Corte Madera, CA: Good Book Publishing Company), pp. 168-69 for illustrations.

We earnestly pray for the right ideal, for guidance in each questionable situation, for sanity, and for strength to do the right thing (p. 70).

We ask that we be given strength and direction to do the right thing, no matter what the personal consequences may be (p. 79).

So we clean house with the family, asking each morning in meditation that our Creator show us the way of patience, tolerance, kindliness and love (p. 83).

How can I best serve Thee—Thy will (not mine) be done (p. 85).

He will show you how to create the fellowship you crave (p. 164).

Ask Him in your morning meditation what you can do each day for the man who is still sick. The answers will come, if your own house is in order (p. 164).

For our group purpose there is but one ultimate authority—a loving God as He may express Himself in our group conscience. Our leaders are but trusted servants; they do not govern (pp. 564-65).

Specific Guidance Ideas
in the Eleventh Step Suggestions

The Big Book devotes several pages to suggestions for practicing the Eleventh Step. All borrow ideas from the Oxford Group and prayer and meditation precepts in the Bible. As previously stated, the Eleventh Step suggestions divide themselves into four categories. But they are preceded by the statement: "Step Eleven suggests prayer and meditation" (p. 85). Merriam Webster's Collegiate Dictionary defines the word "meditate" in transitive sense as: "To focus one's thoughts on: reflect on or ponder over."[13] It is fair to say that meditation on the Bible means focusing one's thoughts on its contents. Meditation on devotionals and other "helpful books" involves a focus on their contents. And meditation involving communion with God would similarly involve focussing on, praying to, and hearing from Him. Following are the Big Book's specific Eleventh Step suggestions:

On Retiring at Night

This Eleventh Step segment calls for a constructive review of the day (p. 86). The "meditation" is really on how well the principles of the Tenth Step were practiced during the day. The Tenth Step suggestions involved a continuing moral inventory of resentments, selfishness, dishonesty, and fear that cropped up during the day (p. 84); and these were all manifestations of self-centeredness that were decried by the Oxford Group. Next, the Tenth Step called on God for help, for confession, for restitution, and for work with others (p. 84)—which also were Oxford Group ideas. In its review of the Tenth Step "day," the Eleventh Step then calls for a request for God's forgiveness where one has fallen short (p. 86). This particular suggestion necessarily involved *prayer for forgiveness*—resting on the provisions of James 5:15 and 1 John 1:7-9—an idea and verses well known to the Oxford Group:[14] The verses read:

> And the prayer of faith shall save the sick, and the Lord shall raise him up; and if he have committed sins, they shall be forgiven him (James 5:15).

> But if we walk in the light, as he [God] is in the light, we have fellowship one with another, and the blood of Jesus Christ his son cleanseth us from all sin (1 John 1:7).

---

[13] *Merriam Webster's Collegiate Dictionary*, 10th ed. (Springfield, MA: Merriam-Webster, 1993).

[14] See Dick B., *The Good Book and The Big Book*, pp. 101-02, 153.

If we confess our sins, he [God] is faithful and just to forgive us *our* sins, and to cleanse us from all unrighteousness (1 John 1:9).

The evening suggestions of the Eleventh Step conclude with the statement that the AA should then inquire of God "what corrective measures should be taken" (p. 86). And Oxford Group people very definitely believed that restitution and the righting of wrongs should be undertaken *with* God's guidance. Thus Oxford Group activist Garth Lean wrote:

God said I must apologise and restore as far as I was able. There was no escaping it. God's searchlight beam kept playing upon them [his mistakes]. This action was for me as definite a test as Christ's command to the blind man to bathe his eyes in the pool of Siloam or to the rich young ruler to sell all he had.[15]

On Awakening

For many AAs today, the Eleventh Step seems mostly to be about prayer and meditation which takes place *on arising* at the beginning of the day. And most of the Big Book suggestions as to what is to be done "on awakening" are very similar to the practices followed by Sam Shoemaker and other Oxford Group people. These we have covered in much detail; so we will merely *summarize* here the A.A. debt as reflected in Big Book language.

The Big Book speaks of laying out plans for the day and asking God to direct one's thinking (p. 86). This approach is mirrored in Shoemaker's "Good Morning" radio broadcast quoted at the beginning of this title. Next, the Big Book speaks of *indecision* and the need for asking God for inspiration, an intuitive thought or a decision (p. 86). And there was much talk in Oxford Group

[15] Garth Lean, *Cast out Your Nets: Sharing Your Faith with Others* (London: Grosvenor, 1990), p. 87.

writings about "intuitive" thinking.[16] Anne Smith stated in her journal: "Guidance comes through direct intuitive thought."[17]

Talking about *how* to receive the "intuitive thought," the Big Book calls for relaxing, taking it easy, and not struggling (p. 86). These same ideas can be found in the Biblical and Oxford Group materials we discussed above. Anne Smith covers this same ground in her journal.[18]

This "morning watch" segment of the Big Book concludes: "We usually conclude the period of meditation with a prayer that we be shown all through the day what our next step is to be, that we be given whatever we need to take care of such problems" (p. 87). The Oxford Group's Victor Kitchen (one of Bill Wilson's friends and businessmen's team colleagues) wrote:

> Where I used to plan the day, making a list of all the jobs I thought I had to finish, all the people I thought I had to see, all 'phone calls I thought I had to make and all the letters I thought I had to write, I now simply ask God's guidance on the day.[19]

Pursuing Spiritual Growth

The author has often called this Big Book Eleventh Step segment the "lost paragraph" because it seems to have been forgotten and is seldom discussed in meetings.

The paragraph suggests asking wives or friends "to join us in morning meditation" if circumstances warrant (p. 87). This brings to mind Shoemaker's own family convocation as described in his

---

[16] Eleanor Napier Forde, *The Guidance of God* (Oxford: The Oxford Group, 1930), p. 21: "The fourth signpost is an intuitive conviction that a course of action is inherently right, the certainty that, hard as it may be, there can be no other way." See also, Samuel M. Shoemaker, Jr., *Twice-Born Ministers* (New York: Fleming H. Revell, 1929), p. 184; *The Conversion of the Church* (New York: Fleming H. Revell, 1932), pp. 53-55.

[17] Dick B., *Anne Smith's Journal, 1933-1939: A.A.'s Principles of Success* (San Rafael, CA: Paradise Research Publications, 1995), p. 58.

[18] Dick B., *Anne Smith's Journal*, pp. 60-63.

[19] Victor C. Kitchen, *I Was a Pagan* (New York: Harper & Brothers, 1934), p. 122.

"Good Morning" radio broadcast. It also calls up memories of the Quiet Time Dr. Bob's daughter recalled—in which her mother gathered "the guys" in the Smith home each morning for Bible study, prayer, listening, and guidance.

The Big Book also speaks here about membership in religious bodies—something that has almost become a taboo topic in many A.A. meetings (p. 87). Yet the original AAs were gently nudged toward attendance at a religious group, though not all of them did.[20]

Then the Big Book suggests, "There are many helpful books"—a topic we have previously discussed.[21]

Throughout the Day, When Agitated or Doubtful

The final Eleventh Step segment in the Big Book deals with guidance in the face of anxiety. It says: "As we go through the day we pause, when agitated or doubtful, and ask for the right thought or action" (p. 87). And this suggestion for guidance in the face of adversity at once recalls to mind the many Bible verses which were the heart of Oxford Group guidance practices in such situations. The verses include: (1) "Be still, and know that I *am* God" (Psalm 46:10). (2) "Lord, what wilt thou have me to do?" (Acts 9:6). (3) "What shall I do, Lord?" (Acts 22:10). (4) "Speak, Lord; for thy servant heareth" (1 Samuel 3:9). (5) "Thou wilt keep *him* in perfect peace, *whose* mind *is* stayed *on thee*: because he trusteth in thee" (Isaiah 26:3). (6) "Take no thought for [be not anxious about] your life, what ye shall eat, or what ye shall drink; nor yet for your body, what ye shall put on. . . . for Your Heavenly Father knoweth that ye have need of all these things. But

---

[20] See (1) Big Book: p. 28—"Not all of us join religious bodies, but most of us favor such memberships; (2) " *DR. BOB and the Good Oldtimers* (New York: Alcoholics Anonymous World Services, 1980), p. 131—"Important, but not vital, that he [the alcoholic] attend some religious service at least once weekly;" (3) Dick B., *That Amazing Grace: The Role of Clarence and Grace S. in Alcoholics Anonymous* (San Rafael, CA: Paradise Research Publications, 1996), p. 92.

[21] Big Book, p. 87.

seek ye first the kingdom of God, and his righteousness; and all these things shall be added unto you" (Matthew 6:25, 32-33). (7) "Be careful for [anxious about] nothing; but in everything by prayer and supplication with thanksgiving let your requests be made known unto God. And the peace of God, which passeth all understanding, shall keep your hearts and minds through Christ Jesus" (Philippians 4:6-7).

The Big Book concludes with the suggestion that AAs in stress should say to themselves "many times each day 'Thy will be done'" (p. 88). And "Thy will be done"—from the Lord's Prayer in the Sermon on the Mount—was, in many ways, the watchword for Oxford Group surrender.[22]

---

[22] Samuel M. Shoemaker, Jr., *Children of the Second Birth: Being a Narrative of Spiritual Miracles in a City Parish* (New York: Fleming H. Revell, 1927), pp. 175-187. Note that this entire chapter is devoted to "Thy will be done." See Matthew 6:10 and The Layman with a Notebook, *What is the Oxford Group?* (London: Oxford University Press, 1933), p. 48.

7

History to the Rescue

What AAs Can Learn from Their Spiritual Roots

How to Gain a Better Understanding of God

In several other titles, the author discussed and documented the variety of weird concepts of a "god" with absurd names that float around the rooms of A.A. and even pop up in some of its more recent literature.[1] These bizarre ideas—emanating from the A.A. expressions "higher power," a "power greater than ourselves," and "God as we understood Him"—have evolved into names for some "god" who is variously called a "lightbulb," a "chair," a "bulldozer," a "stone," a "tree," "Santa Claus," the "Big Dipper," the "group," "Group Of Drunks," "Good Orderly Direction," the "man upstairs," and *even* "Ralph!" The author has personally heard and read them all. So have many others in and out of A.A.[2] So did A.A.'s venerable Clarence S., who was so

---

[1] See discussion in Dick B., *The Good Book and The Big Book* (San Rafael, CA: Paradise Research Publications, 1995), pp. 53-62.

[2] See Dick B., *The Good Book and The Big Book*, p. 43.

disturbed about the trend that he wrote a pamphlet titled *My Higher Power-The Light Bulb.*[3]

A look at recent A.A. Conference Approved literature will reveal the problem. One pamphlet says: "While some members prefer to call this Power 'God,' we were told that this was purely a matter of personal interpretation; we could conceive of the Power in any terms we thought fit."[4] Another pamphlet designed to inform the "clergy" states: "Some choose the A.A. group as their 'Higher Power'; some look to God—*as they understand Him*; and others rely upon entirely different concepts."[5] Still another declares: "Alcohol had become a power greater than themselves. . . . A. A. suggests that to achieve and maintain sobriety, alcoholics need to accept and depend upon another Power recognized as greater than themselves. Some alcoholics choose to consider the A. A. group itself as the power greater than themselves; for many others, this power is God—*as they, individually, understand Him*; still others rely upon entirely different concepts of a Higher Power."[6] *A Newcomer Asks* tells the reader: "However, everyone defines this power as he or she wishes. Many people call *it* God, others think *it* is the A.A. group, still others don't believe in *it* at all."[7]

However one may appraise these recent developments, the statements are factual. Many represent the "Conference Approved" view of today. Such statements often lead to the suggestion

[3] See Dick B., *That Amazing Grace: The Role of Clarence and Grace S. in Alcoholics Anonymous* (San Rafael, CA: Paradise Research Publications, 1996), pp. 46-50, 89; Clarence S., *My Higher Power: The Light Bulb*, 2d ed. (Winter Park: FL: Dick Stultz, 1981).

[4] *This Is A.A.: An Introduction to the AA Recovery Program* (New York: Alcoholics Anonymous World Services, 1984), p. 15.

[5] *Members of the Clergy Ask about Alcoholics Anonymous*, Rev. 1992 (New York: Alcoholics Anonymous World Services, 1961), p. 13.

[6] *44 Questions* (New York: Alcoholics Anonymous World Services, 1952), p. 19.

[7] *A Newcomer Asks* (A.A. General Service Office, New York), p. 4. The italics were added by the author to the word *it*—an unusual pronoun to be used if one were referring to God Almighty.

addressed to a newcomer "Fake it till you make it." One of the author's younger sponsees is fond of pointing out that he did "fake it" for two years, continued to drink and use, and very definitely did *not* make it until he began relying on "divine help"—something the Big Book suggests as being essential.[8]

A.A.'s own roots—taken from the Bible, according to its co-founder Dr. Bob—make abundantly clear who the "Divine" power was. God—as He is described in the Bible—was that power. He is described in A.A.'s root sources—and still is described in A.A.'s Big Book—as the *Creator* ("Elohim").[9] He is *God Almighty* ("El Shaddai").[10] He is *Lord* ("Jehovah").[11] In the Old Testament, as Jehovah, God "authored" names for Himself which described His relationship with that which He created: *Jehovah-Jireh* (Jehovah will see, or provide); *Jehovah-Ropheka* (Jehovah that healeth thee); *Jehovah-Nissi* (Jehovah my banner); *Jehovah Mckaddishkem* (Jehovah that doth sanctify you); *Jehovah-Shalom* (Jehovah [send] peace); *Jehovah Zebaoth* (Jehovah of hosts); *Jehovah Zidkenu* (Jehovah our righteousness); *Jehovah-Shammah* (Jehovah is there); *Jehovah Elyon* (Jehovah most high); and *Jehovah Roi* (Jehovah my Shepherd).[12] The Twenty-Third Psalm

---

[8] See *Alcoholics Anonymous*, 3rd ed. (New York: Alcoholics Anonymous World Services, 1976), p. 43: "As to two of you men, there is no doubt in my mind that you were 100% hopeless apart from divine help."

[9] Isaiah 40:18 (compare Genesis 1:1); Andrew Jukes, *The Names of God in Holy Scripture* (Grand Rapids, MI: Kregel Publications, 1967), pp. 15-34; Harold Begbie, *Life Changers* (London: Mills and Boon, Ltd., 1923), p. 20; Big Book, pp. 13, 25, 28, 56, 68, 72, 75, 76, 80, 158, 161.

[10] Genesis 17:1; 35:11; Exodus 6:3; Ezekiel 10:5; Jukes, *The Names of God*, pp. 59-82. And Bill Wilson so described Him. See Dick B., *The Akron Genesis of Alcoholics Anonymous* (Corte Madera, CA: Good Book Publishing Company, 1994), pp. 12-13.

[11] Jukes, *The Names of God*, pp. 35-58.

[12] See Appendix 4 of *The Companion Bible: The Authorized Version of 1611 with the Structures and Critical, Explanatory, and Suggestive Notes and with 198 Appendices* (Grand Rapids, MI: Kregel Publications, 1990), p. 6.

was widely read and used in early A.A.[13] And seven of the foregoing "Jehovah" titles are referred to in Psalm 23.[14]

The point is that early AAs were familiar with the attributes of God *as God described Himself in the Bible.* God called Himself the Creator. He called Himself God Almighty. He called Himself Lord; and He described what He did as Creator in providing, healing, protecting, sanctifying, sending peace, being the Shepherd, and so on. As they prayed and meditated on God's Word, and listened for His directions, early AAs were not praying to a chair, a lightbulb, or a group. They were praying to the God *with* power and with a power God Himself *described.* A.A.'s Biblical roots can help AAs today to gain an understanding of God if they so desire; and, with that understanding, the AA can pray with assurance and with an understanding of the loving, providing God to whom the prayers are addressed.

For good measure, we should add that God further describes Himself in the New Testament in such a way that prayer to a bulldozer is excluded and prayer to the kind of source one would want is surely invited. God is Spirit.[15] God is "the living God."[16] God is the God of peace, the God of grace, the God of patience and consolation, the God of hope, the God of all comfort, the Father of mercies, and the God of love.[17] And the descriptions were nothing new to early AAs. Bill Wilson, Dr. Bob, and Anne Smith all referred to God as the God of love.[18] That concept is clear in A.A.'s Big Book and in its Twelve Traditions.

---

[13] See, for example, Dick B., *That Amazing Grace*, pp. 41, 96-97; *A Manual for Alcoholics Anonymous*, 6th rev. ed. (Akron, Ohio: AA of Akron, 1989), p. 8.

[14] See *The Companion Bible*, Appendix 4, p. 6.

[15] John 4:24; Big Book, p. 84.

[16] Matthew 16:16; Acts 14:15; Romans 9:26; 1 Timothy 3:15; 4:10. Hebrews 9:14; 10:31. Compare the language in Big Book, p. 28.

[17] Romans 16:20; 1 Peter 5:10; Romans 15:5; Romans 15:13; 2 Corinthians 1:3; 1 John 4:8, 16.

[18] Big Book, pp. 564-65; *DR. BOB and the Good Oldtimers* (Alcoholics Anonymous World Services, Inc., 1980), p. 110; Dick B., *Anne Smith's Journal, 1933-1939: A.A.'s Principles of Success* (San Rafael, CA: Paradise Research Publications, 1994), pp. 4, 15.

Prayer to some dead god (a tree or a chair) for healing and deliverance simply was not made in early A.A.; nor to a visible god (a lightbulb or a bulldozer); nor to a god of temptation and trouble (involving, for example, a disaster "given" by God to "teach us a lesson").[19]

Where to Look for Knowledge of God's Universal Will and of His Particular Will

Gone can be the starry-eyed confusion one often hears in A.A. meetings today about the quandary of God's will. History makes clear that one need not pray for the knowledge of most of what God proclaims to be His will. The bulk of God's will is set forth with clarity in the Bible. A.A.'s root sources made it clear that one needs to be a child of God to be able to understand the will of God. One certainly needs to *study* the word of God to know the will of God. One often needs to pray in order to gain understanding of the word of God. And one may need "helpful books," clergy, and church to learn about the Bible, how to study it, and how to become a child of God.

Bill Wilson himself said this about "guidance":

While most of us believe profoundly in the principle of "guidance," it was soon apparent that to receive it accurately, *considerable spiritual preparation was necessary* (italics added).[20]

Bill's comments echoed the beliefs of the Oxford Group and of Dr. Bob. One needed to study Scripture and check "guidance" against Scripture to see if thoughts received squared with the "universal" or "general" will of God. One needed to know and study the

---

[19] See James 1:12-18. Recall that the Book of James was a favorite among early AAs—a fact often discussed in A.A. Conference Approved histories. See *DR. BOB*, p. 71; *Pass It On: The Story of Bill Wilson and How the A.A. Message Reached the World* (New York: Alcoholics Anonymous World Services, Inc., 1984), p. 147.

[20] *Pass It On*, p. 172.

"Four Absolutes" to check thoughts against the teachings of Jesus as the Oxford Group believed them to be embodied in the Absolutes. One needed to consult an experienced believer when he or she found himself in the soup over some thought received. These were sound rules. They were long-standing precepts. And they were designed to preclude what Sam Shoemaker called "half-baked" prayers and "self-made" religion.[21] Interestingly, though, Bill may also have been referring at that point in A.A. to some Roman Catholic ideas that "guidance" necessitated involvement by the "Church" itself.

Receiving knowledge of the will of God, then, does not merely involve a plea to "Intuit me. Intuit me." The will of God can be learned from the Word of God and, if the thoughts are consistent with the Word and for profit, from God's revelation to His children. Considerable spiritual preparation *is* necessary; and that is why the Big Book's Tenth and Eleventh Step suggestions spoke of spiritual *growth* (pp. 84-85). That is why Bill Wilson spoke of A.A. itself as a *spiritual kindergarten*.[22] That is why early AAs studied Scripture.

How, Why, and When to Study Ancillary Books

As we have said, A.A.'s Big Book speaks of the value, in meditation and devotions, of "helpful books" (p. 87). Anne Smith made similar recommendations in her spiritual journal.[23] She specifically recommended several books on the life of Jesus Christ.[24] Dr. Bob and others studied several books which helped

---

[21] For a detailed discussion of Shoemaker's views and the places where they can be found, see Dick B., *The Good Book and The Big Book*, pp. 184-85; *New Light on Alcoholism: The A.A. Legacy from Sam Shoemaker* (Corte Madera, CA: Good Book Publishing Company, 1994), pp. 219, 303-04.

[22] See Dick B., *The Good Book and The Big Book*, p. 188, n. 30.

[23] See Dick B., *Anne Smith's Journal*, pp. 79-85.

[24] James Stalker, *The Life of Jesus Christ* (New York: Fleming H. Revell, 1891); Robert E. Speer, *Studies of the Man Christ Jesus* (New York: Fleming H. Revell, 1896); T. R. Glover, *The Jesus of History* (New York: Association Press, 1930).

to explain the Sermon on the Mount (Matthew 5-7).[25] Dr. Bob, Anne, and others studied books that aided in understanding 1 Corinthians 13.[26] Glenn Clark, whose books were favorites of Dr. Bob's, wrote *The Lord's Prayer and Other Talks on Prayer from The Camps Farthest Out.*[27] *The Runner's Bible*, another book popular with Dr. Bob and some early AAs, listed groups of Bible verses under topics dealing with God, thankfulness, overcoming fear, and so on.[28] Roger Hicks, an Oxford Group writer and activist (who was present in Akron, Ohio, during A.A.'s earliest formative days) wrote a pamphlet *How to Read the Bible.*[29] Frank Buchman hired a Miss Mary Angevine as a Bible teacher to *teach* Bible to the Oxford Group businessmen's team of which Bill Wilson was a part; and Miss Angevine also taught Bible at Oxford Group houseparties probably attended by Bill.[30] Bill Wilson credited Shoemaker's assistant minister, the Reverend W. Irving Harris, with many of the ideas early AAs obtained.[31] And the author has in his possession a number articles and pamphlets Harris wrote on the Bible and prayer.[32] Harris himself pointed out, in his biography of Sam Shoemaker, that Shoemaker's Calvary Church "was a place to learn the how of faith, both in sermons and in groups—How to find God. How to pray. How to

---

[25] E. Stanley Jones, *The Christ of the Mount* (New York: Abingdon Press, 1930); Oswald Chambers, *Studies in the Sermon on the Mount* (London: Simpkin, Marshall, n.d.); Emmet Fox, *The Sermon on the Mount* (New York: Harper & Row, 1934).

[26] Henry Drummond, *Essays and Addresses* (London: James Potts & Co., 1904)—which included the famous address, *The Greatest Thing in the World*; Toyohiko Kagawa, *Love: The Law of Life* (Philadelphia: The John C. Winston Co., 1929).

[27] Glenn Clark, *The Lord's Prayer and Other Talks on Prayer from The Camps Farthest Out* (Minnesota: Macalester Publishing Co., 1932).

[28] Nora Smith Holm, *The Runner's Bible* (New York: Houghton Mifflin Company, 1915).

[29] Roger Hicks, *How to Read the Bible: Notes for Revolutionaries* (London: The Oxford Group, n.d.).

[30] See Dick B., *The Akron Genesis of Alcoholics Anonymous*, pp. 29, 175-76.

[31] See Dick B., *New Light on Alcoholism*, p. 259.

[32] E.g., W. Irving Harris, *An Outline of the Life of Christ* (New York: The Oxford Group, 1935).

read the Bible. How to pass faith on."[33] Shoemaker himself wrote many articles on how to study the Bible.[34]

The "helpful books" of early A.A., then, were not merely the one-page inspirational notes for the day as exemplified by *The Upper Room* and *My Utmost for His Highest*. They were frequently books to *aid in understanding the entire Bible*, and major topics in the Bible (such as the Sermon on the Mount, the Lord's Prayer, 1 Corinthians 13, prayer, healing, and thankfulness).

An *hour* of quiet time with early AAs and their progenitors was scarcely enough! There was a great deal of study material to go with it and to help in its implementation.

The key to early A.A. Bible study, prayer, meditation, and listening was not reliance on some ancillary book for a brief morning pit-stop with God. Our title should make that fact clear. The "meditation" books of early AAs were simply spurs to further prayer or study on a particular subject. And the best of these meditation books referred to specific Bible verses and to specific Bible segments for further study. Such *ancillary books* can be of *help* today, but *not as substitutes* for the work early AAs did in the Bible itself, in prayer, and in quiet listening.

What to Do to Receive the Power of God

A.A. today is *not* a Christian fellowship. Not a society which requires a statement of faith. Early "membership" requirements were later dropped in favor of no "membership" at all. The A.A. of today simply suggests that a "desire to stop drinking" is enough to start with.

We do not need to cover the ground already trod. Suffice it to quote Scripture, Shoemaker, the Oxford Group writings, and some of the other religious literature of early A. A. to make it clear that

---

[33] W. Irving Harris, *The Breeze of the Spirit* (New York: The Seabury Press, 1978), pp. 25, 18.

[34] For examples, see Dick B., *Design for Living: The Oxford Group's Contribution to Early A.A.* (San Rafael, CA: Paradise Research Publications, 1995), pp. 250-52.

in A.A.'s early days the power of God was, for almost all of the AAs, received through acceptance of Jesus Christ as one's personal Lord and Saviour.

In John 3:3, Jesus taught: "Except a man be born again, he cannot see the kingdom of God." In John 3:5, Jesus said: "Except a man be born of water and *of* the spirit, he cannot enter into the kingdom of God." In John 3:7, he stated again, "Marvel not that I said unto thee, Ye must be born again." In John 14:6, he finalized the point by saying: "I am the way, the truth, and the life; no man cometh unto the Father, but by me."[35]

Jesus's last words, as recorded in Luke 24:49, were: "And, behold, I send the promise of My Father upon you: but tarry *ye* in the city of Jerusalem, until ye be endued with power from on high." Following instructions, the Apostles were ready on the day of Pentecost: "And they were all filled with the Holy Ghost. . . ."[36] And, after Peter and John had healed the man at the gate of the temple, they were asked, "By what power, or by what name, have *ye* done this?"[37] Peter's reply was:

> If *we* this day be examined of the good deed done to the impotent man, by what means *he* is made whole; Be it known unto you all, and to all the people of Israel, that by the name of Jesus Christ of Nazareth, Whom *ye* crucified, Whom God raised from the dead, *even* by *him* doth this man stand before you whole. . . . Neither is there salvation in any other: for there is none other name under heaven given among men, whereby we must be saved.[38]

Sam Shoemaker, and the other Oxford Group writers who influenced early A.A. thinking, *all* taught that—to receive the power of God—you must be reborn. And Bill Wilson himself so

---

[35] See Dick B., *That Amazing Grace*, p. 52.

[36] Acts 2:4.

[37] Acts 4:7.

[38] Acts 4:9-10, 12.

believed at the earliest days of his sobriety.[39] Thus, whatever the
AAs of today may wish to believe, and whatever they wish to call
a god, the earliest AAs were clear that the power of God was
received through a new birth.[40]

The Nature and Specifics of God's Instructions on Prayer

Quite often, one hears in an A.A. meeting that a person's prayer
is "kept simple." The AA may say, "I just ask Him for help in the
morning, and thank Him at night." Yet there is no suggestion that
this was the kind of prayer utilized in early A.A. or called for in
the Bible. Similarly, an unusual suggestion is made in the Big
Book which is often taken out of context and seems to suggest that
one may *never* pray for himself or herself.[41] As to such an idea,
Shoemaker said:

> Does this mean, then, that we can never pray for ourselves or
> for "things?" By no means! Someone told me the other day that
> he never prays for himself. I told him that I frequently needed to
> pray for myself—not to get what I want, but to be what I ought,
> and to re-align myself with God's will. I need forgiveness, I
> need grace, I need direction. But the objective is not my
> pleasure, but the quality of my service.[42]

---

[39] Samuel M. Shoemaker, Jr., *Twice-Born Ministers* (New York: Fleming H. Revell,
1929), pp. 56, 10; Begbie, *Life Changers*, p. 104; Geoffrey Francis Allen, *He That
Cometh* (New York: The Macmillan Company, 1933), pp. 19, 32, 48. For other
citations, see Dick B., *Design for Living*, p. 277. For the record of Bill Wilson's own
statements that he had "been born again," see Dick B., *New Light on Alcoholism*, p. 55,
n. 10.

[40] See Dick B., *That Amazing Grace*, pp. 25-27, 33-34.

[41] The actual text of the Big Book states: "We ask especially for freedom from self
will, and are careful to make no request for ourselves only. We may ask for ourselves,
however, if others will be helped. We are careful never to pray for our own selfish ends"
(p. 87).

[42] Samuel M. Shoemaker, Jr., *How to Find God* (New York: Faith at Work, n.d.),
p. 12.

One could go a good deal further than Shoemaker did. The Psalms, for example, are filled with prayers for deliverance from fear, from danger, and from trouble.[43] If one looks at John 10:10 and 3 John 2, it is apparent that God promises and makes available the abundant, prosperous, and healthy life. Anne Smith specifically commented on this in her spiritual journal.[44] In other words, it is certainly available to pray for the more than abundant, prosperous, and healthy life.

The New Testament quite specifically talks of asking in the name of Jesus Christ.[45] The Bible says to ask according to God's will.[46] To ask with thanksgiving.[47] To ask with believing.[48] And we have already discussed that prayers may involve adoration and praise, thanksgiving, intercession, forgiveness, the meeting of needs, healing, guidance, and so on.

When the Bible offers a storehouse of promises that God says He will perform (and also offers specific instructions on how to ask), there is certainly no need for a "simple" prayer that asks for help in the morning. Most of us need help all day long—overcoming fear, seeking guidance, giving thanks, avoiding anxiety, gaining peace, claiming healing, asking forgiveness, and helping others. And the Word of God contains verses, examples, and directions pertaining to each of these. It has been said that there are over 900 promises in the Word of God which are available for God's kids to claim. If we simply returned to the Twenty-Third and Ninety-First Psalms, which early AAs used with

---

[43] See, for example, Psalm 34:4; Psalm 103:4; Psalm 91:15.

[44] Dick B., *Anne Smith's Journal*, pp. 71, 131.

[45] John 14:13-14; John 16:23-24, 26. See also, Glenn Clark, *The Soul's Sincere Desire* (Boston: Little, Brown and Company, 1927), pp. 63-86; Holm, *The Runner's Bible*, pp. 37, 60, 64; Shoemaker, *How to Find God*, pp. 11-12.

[46] 1 John 5:14-15; Holm, *The Runner's Bible*, p. 64; Glenn Clark, *I Will Lift Up Mine Eyes* (New York; Harper & Brothers, 1937), p. 24.

[47] Philippians 4:6-7; Holm, *The Runner's Bible*, pp. 61, 115, 147, 155; Harry Emerson Fosdick, *The Meaning of Prayer* (New York: Association Press, 1934), p. 72; Clark, *I Will Lift Up Mine Eyes*, p. 93.

[48] James 1:6; Mark 9:23; Mark 11:24; Holm, *The Runner's Bible*, pp. 41-45, 51.

such frequency, we can see how much can be involved in prayer
to a loving God. In fact, the Psalms are filled with examples of
effective prayers that were used by King David himself.

A person entering a room filled with good things intended for
him would hardly want to look in just one drawer, conclude there
is nothing else, and leave with unfilled needs! Quiet time with
Bible study, books, prayer, listening, and checking could and can
be a time-consuming *and* rewarding endeavor if one knows where
and how to look for God's promises.

The Meaning of Meditation

Much of the confusion over "meditation" could be eliminated if
one looked in a good dictionary for a definition of the word
"meditation." Then looked in the Bible to see what people there
"meditated" on and about. And then looked at the very substantial
practices early AAs and their forbears used to get in touch *with*
God, study *about* Him, pray *to* Him, listen *for* His "Voice," and
then verify the authenticity of a message believed to be *from* Him.

The Deliverance That Can Come from Quiet Time with God

If the testimony of the Bible means anything at all, it certainly
affirms the existence of God and the power of God. It affirms His
availability for healing, forgiveness, and deliverance.[49] It affirms
His goodness and the nature of the gifts He gives (James 1:17). It
affirms His offers of guidance.[50] It affirms that He will do above
and beyond all that we can ask or think.[51] It affirms the need for,
and superiority of, His power over the power of the god of this

---

[49] Psalm 103.

[50] Psalm 32:8; Proverbs 3:5-6.

[51] Ephesians 3:20. Miles G. W. Phillimore, *Just for Today* (privately published
pamphlet, 1940), pp. 8-9.

world.[52] And it affirms that God *is* a God of peace and will keep in perfect peace the mind of the believer which is stayed on Him and His word.[53]

The Trek from Spiritual Kindergarten to Spiritual Maturity

Beginnings in the Eleventh Step

Countless times, Bill Wilson expressed the idea that A.A. was a *spiritual kindergarten.*[54] A.A.'s Big Book states, in its discussion of the Eleventh Step: "Be quick to see where religious people are right. Make use of what they have to offer" (p. 87). And the very language of the Eleventh Step suggests the importance of *seeking and improvement*—"Sought through prayer and meditation to improve . . . "

The author believes the Eleventh Step approach in A.A.'s Big Book can be divided, for discussion purposes, into four parts: (1) Suggestions for what to do on retiring at night. (2) Suggestions for what to do on awakening. (3) Suggestions for spiritual growth through prayer, meditation, study of books, membership in a religious denomination, and the assistance of clergy. (4) Suggestions for meeting the stresses and anxieties that arise throughout the day. The suggestions are covered in less than two-and-a-half pages of the Big Book (pp. 85-88). If one compares these pages to the many pages of the Bible which discuss prayer, or the many prayer books which exist to aid prayer, or the many writings which AAs themselves read about prayer, it is obvious

---

[52] John 10:10; Romans, Chapter 8: Ephesians, Chapter 6; 1 John 4:4: "*Ye* are of God, little children, and have overcome them: because greater is He that is in you, than he that is in the world."

[53] Romans 15:33; Isaiah 26:3.

[54] See Dick B., *The Good Book and The Big Book*, p. 188, n. 30; *New Light on Alcoholism*, pp. 12-13; *As Bill Sees It: The A.A. Way of Life . . . selected writings of A.A.'s co-founder* (New York: Alcoholics Anonymous World Services, Inc.), p. 45.

that the Big Book is merely a guide as to how to *approach* "prayer and meditation." The Big Book is not, and does not purport to be, a compendium on prayer.

Early AAs were readers![55] The number of books they read for spiritual growth was quite large.[56] And one must add to these books the many daily Bible devotionals in wide circulation in the pioneer days—books and pamphlets such as *The Upper Room, My Utmost For His Highest, Victorious Living, Daily Strength for Daily Living, The Runner's Bible,* and *The Meaning of Prayer.*

All these resources had their place in the thinking of those who knew they did not, on their own, have all the spiritual answers. When they emerged from the fog of alcoholism, early AAs were introduced to the Bible at once. They were also handed a copy of *The Upper Room.* And, if they chose to, they were introduced by Dr. Bob, Anne Smith, Henrietta Seiberling, and others to books for religious growth, such as *As a Man Thinketh, In His Steps, The Greatest Thing in the World, The Sermon on the Mount, The Varieties of Religious Experience,* and a host of others, including the many utilized or written by Oxford Group people.

Should AAs begin with any less today?

Growth through the Guidance of God

The previous segment focused on *books* as an aid to spiritual learning and growth in Quiet Time. An equally important aspect is the guidance of God Himself.

The essence of prayer and meditation practices in Quiet Time was *communion* with God Almighty. A.A. speaks of improving one's *conscious contact* with God.[57] A.A. and its Oxford Group

---

[55] See Foreword by Dr. Ernest Kurtz in Dick B., *Dr. Bob's Library: Books for Twelve Step Growth* (San Rafael, CA: Paradise Research Publications, 1994).

[56] See Dick B., *The Books Early AAs Read for Spiritual Growth,* 6th ed. (Kihei, HI: Paradise Research Publications, Inc., 1998).

[57] Big Book, p. 59.

mentors spoke of attaining a *spiritual experience.*[58] Thus, great stock was placed in what man could do directly with God through speaking and listening to Him. Two-way prayer, the Oxford Group called it. And we have covered the many verses in the Bible which show that God has spoken to man throughout the ages. God has revealed Himself to man through the words of the Bible, through tongues with interpretation and prophecy, through direct revelation, and through phenomena.

The burning bush was the exception. Communications to and from God were the norm. And they can be today. Hence, in A.A.'s roots, spiritual growth *began* in books—in Bible study and the ancillary reading. But it *progressed daily* through reaching out to God via prayer and listening.

Should AAs seek growth through lesser means today?

Deliverance through the Power of God

Sometimes one gains the impression in A.A. meetings that the only solution offered by the Twelve Steps is the elimination of drinking. But a glance at the Big Book will show that the inference is wrong. "Our liquor was but a symptom," says the Big Book (p. 64). "Bottles were only a symbol," adds the Big Book (p. 103). The real problem, states the Big Book, is the "spiritual disease"—the "spiritual malady," the fact that "we [alcoholics] have been spiritually sick" (p. 64).

Shoemaker addressed that problem in his first title:

Whatever misery persons of the present day might experience within the ranks of religion, one cannot see that many of them are faring much better outside. . . . Now the thing which is striking about much of the misery one sees is that it is *spiritual* misery. It is the unhappiness of *spiritual* people very often—souls who are too fine-grained to get along without religion, yet who have never come to terms with it. It is the maladjustment to the

---

[58] Shoemaker, *Twice Born Ministers*, pp. 10, 61; Big Book, pp. 47, 569.

eternal things, and this throws out the whole focus of life. Rest
cures and exercise and motor drives will not help. The only thing
that will help is religion. For the root of the malady is
estrangement from God—estrangement from Him in people that
were made to be His companions. . . . What you want is simply
a vital religious experience. You need to find God. You need
Jesus Christ.[59]

Addressing this theme, A.A.'s Big Book states:

But there is One who has all power—that One is God. May you
find Him now (p. 59)!

My friend [Bill Wilson's friend, Ebby T.] promised when these
things [the Oxford Group's life-changing "Steps"] were done I
would enter upon a new relationship with my Creator; that I
would have the elements of a way of living which answered *all
my problems* (p. 13, italics added).

Lack of power, that was our dilemma. We had to find a power
by which we could live. . . . Well, that's exactly what this book
is about. Its main object is to enable you to find a Power greater
than yourself which will solve *your problem [lack of power]*.
That means we have written a book which we believe to be
spiritual as well as moral. And it means, of course, that we are
going to talk about God (p. 45, italics added).

Which returns us to A.A.'s spiritual roots.
Jesus Christ promised those Jews which believed on Him:

If *ye* continue in my word, *then* are ye my disciples indeed: And
ye shall know the truth, and the truth shall make you free. . . .
If the Son therefore shall make you free, ye shall be free indeed
(John 8:31-32, 36).[60]

---

[59] Samuel M. Shoemaker, *Realizing Religion* (New York: Association Press, 1923),
pp. 4-5, 9.
[60] See Holm, *The Runner's Bible*, p. 46.

> . . . ye shall receive power, after that the Holy Ghost is come
> upon you: and ye shall be witnesses unto me both in Jerusalem,
> and in all Judaea, and in Samaria, and unto the uttermost part of
> the earth (Acts 1:8).[61]

And there were the admonitions about the source of power:

> Jesus answered and said unto them, Ye do err, not knowing the
> scriptures, nor the power of God (Matthew 22:29).[62]

> For I am not ashamed of the gospel of Christ: for it is the power
> of God unto salvation to everyone that believeth; to the Jew first,
> and also to the Greek (Romans 1:16).

Anne Smith wrote in her journal:

> Paul speaks of a wish toward good, but power to carry it out is
> lacking. A stronger power than his was needed. God provided
> the power through Christ, so that we could find a new kind of
> relationship with God. Christ gives the power, we appropriate it.
> It is not anything that we do ourselves; but it is the appropriation
> of a power that comes from God that saves us from sin and sets
> us free [p. 37 of Anne Smith's Journal].[63]

Should AAs settle for any less power than this today?

Suggestions from the Author's Experience in A.A.

We need to start with several observations about A.A.; and they
are observations which anyone presently active in, and familiar
with, our Fellowship can make.

---

[61] Samuel M. Shoemaker, "Spiritual Power: The Force Which Makes Life Different," in *Sam Shoemaker at His Best: Extraordinary Living for the Ordinary Man* (New York: Faith At Work, 1964), p. 113.

[62] See Holm, *The Runner's Bible*, p. 51.

[63] Dick B., *Anne Smith's Journal*, p. 22.

First, the impact of A.A. is enormous. There are some two million "members" around the world today. About a million can be found in the United States, and another million elsewhere around the globe. You can find an A.A. office, meeting, or contact almost anywhere you travel in the United States. The author has attended A.A. meetings in the States of Hawaii, California, Washington, Minnesota, Wisconsin, Ohio, Kentucky, West Virginia, New York, Rhode Island, and Vermont. He has attended them in several different cities in most of those states. He has personally met AAs he knows: In banks, service stations, airports, office buildings, restaurants, ticket booths, legal offices, doctors' offices, copy centers, taxi-cabs, elevators, jails, prisons, probation offices, fast-food establishments, department stores, merchandise centers, and street corners. He has received phone calls from AAs living in many distant areas of the United States—and phone calls, faxes, and Email messages from still more. The contacts have not been sought to rack up a record. The author is not a "Conference Speaker," nor a delegate, nor an A.A. staff employee. Most of the contacts have occurred as part of his regular day's walk in sobriety and writing.

Second, A.A. is not lacking in countless individual groups and meetings in well-populated areas. In the author's home county in California, there were over three hundred meetings a week. In Maui, where his office is located, there appear to be more than forty a week. He has often attended A.A. meetings in hospitals, jails, sober clubs, and recovery centers.

Third, the A.A. of today is not lacking in people who believe in God, nor in those who attend religious bodies, spiritual gatherings, and Bible fellowships. In fact, the author has seldom posed to an A.A. newcomer the question: "Do you believe in God?" without receiving an affirmative answer. With that said, however, some other observations are appropriate.

It is no secret that A.A.'s success rate today is far, far below that in its earliest years. Next, one need only attend a "birthday" or "chip" meeting to see how few people respond when calls are made for those with substantial sobriety to identify themselves.

Moreover, the diversity of sources pouring people into A.A.—courts, counselors, recovery centers, clergy, interventionists, physicians, and therapists—certainly results in a diversity of ideas as to what A.A. is all about. In addition, the Big Book has ceased to be the only text for recovery within the Fellowship. People are seeking later books written by Bill Wilson; literature published by recovery programs; and pamphlets published by diversely situated AAs. Finally, A.A.'s original emphasis on belief in God, the Bible, and Christian precepts is simply *gone!* A.A. and AAs (by and large) are quick to state today that their program is "spiritual, not religious."[64] This, despite the fact that they probably cannot define the difference and do not know the difference—if there is one.[65]

You can state factually that A.A. is not in danger of being converted to Christianity. You can state emphatically it is not in danger of adopting some particular sectarian or denominational creed. And the author has had three recent experiences that demonstrate the latter point.

First, a short time ago, a young AA attended a young people's meeting the author was attending. This young man had given a substantial period of his early sobriety to attending A.A. meetings regularly, studying the Big Book, and taking the Twelve Steps of recovery. At this particular meeting, the young man shared his joy about a new experience in religion. He said he had met a group of Christians who had interested him in a church and had given him a new spiritual direction in his life. Abruptly, his sharing of this experience was interrupted by a man who announced angrily that he was a "Hindu," that he was "offended" by the young man's remarks, and that he (the Hindu) had some strong beliefs about God (which he then shared for about ten minutes).

---

[64] See Ernest Kurtz, *Not-God: A History of Alcoholics Anonymous*, exp. ed. (Center City, MN: Hazelden Educational Materials, 1991), pp. 194-95; Ernest Kurtz and Katherine Ketcham, *The Spirituality of Imperfection: Modern Wisdom from Classic Stories* (New York: Bantam Books, 1992), p. 209.

[65] See discussion of this point in Mel B., *New Wine: The Spiritual Roots of the Twelve Step Miracle* (Center City, MN: Hazelden Educational Materials, 1991), pp. 4-5.

The Hindu's diatribe was followed by the remarks of an oldtimer with twenty or more years of sobriety. The oldtimer proclaimed, with seeming satisfaction, that he attended a nearby Roman Catholic church where he took care of his religious needs. He said he came to A.A. *only* "to learn about his alcoholism." And he declared that the two should be kept separate. The Roman Catholic's comments were seconded by those of a Protestant oldtimer with over twenty-five years of sobriety.

The very next person to share was a man who said he had been sober for over seventeen years. He stated he was grossly annoyed at "the Christian nature of meetings in Hawaii." He said he was becoming involved in Judaism and was constantly being pelted with "anti-Semitic" statements at A.A. meetings. Just where those remarks were being made was not at all clear. But the author thinks it safe to say that none of the above four men is in jeopardy of having to adopt the Bible study, prayer, or quiet time practices that prevailed in early A.A.

Just the other day, the author attended a "speaker" meeting where an A.A. dinosaur with almost fifty years of sobriety was holding forth for an hour. Then the oldtimer was asked about "religion" problems. The man responded by panning the "Unity" Church to which he had formerly belonged. Not only was this a violation of A.A. Traditions, it was a flagrant example of how quick AAs today are to criticize "religion" and extol the virtues of "spirituality." And when the author asked the old gentleman how he defined "spiritual," the circumlocution finally ended with the statement that it was the absence of "stinking thinking."

The problem is that one is hard-put in A.A. today to find any mention of the nature of God, the ingredients of His will, the attributes and objectives of prayer to Him, the scope of His healing and delivering power, techniques for listening to Him, or places to go for literature on spiritual growth. The author's experience is that such discussions rarely occur today without being accompanied by criticism of "religion," criticism of the mention of "God," or declarations that neither the Bible nor Christianity should be mentioned in an A.A. meeting.

Consider what Bill W. said in the Big Book of one *real* alcoholic: "ever more serious alcoholism, impending mental and physical collapse," and disillusionment which "brought him [that person] to the point of self-destruction" (p. 56). Bill also wrote: "All of us felt at times that we were regaining control, but such intervals—usually brief—were inevitably followed by still less control, which led in time to pitiful and incomprehensible demoralization" (p. 30). Lastly, he wrote:

> The less people tolerated us, the more we withdrew from society, from life itself. As we became subjects of King Alcohol, shivering denizens of his mad realm, the chilling vapor that is loneliness settled down. It thickened, ever becoming blacker. Some of us sought out sordid places, hoping to find understanding companionship and approval. Momentarily we did—then would come oblivion and the awful awakening to face the hideous Four Horsemen—Terror, Bewilderment, Frustration, Despair. Unhappily drinkers who read this page will understand (p. 151).

The foregoing graphic descriptions of an alcoholic "bottom" depict the author's own experience. Not just his experience with alcoholism and early recovery, but his experience in listening to some fifty or more First and Fifth Step "confessions" by men he has sponsored. Many more such descriptions can be heard in more general terms at good A.A. meetings. Others are contained in stories recounted in the various editions of the Big Book itself.

The Solution

And now for the solution.

The author particularly admires one A.A. oldtimer in California who has sponsored a great many men. The man today has about twenty years of sobriety. He often shares about God, the Big Book, the Twelve Steps, and sponsorship; and the men he sponsors appear recovered and healthy. That man has always been very honest in describing the calls he makes to *his* sponsor. He tells the story that his sponsor usually reproves his complaints by saying, "Three and Eleven, Jack." The man never explained the "Three and Eleven" remark. But the author has a hunch about its meaning. Jack's sponsor was telling him in substance: (1) In Step Three, you made a decision to quit playing God, to let God be God, and to turn your life over to *His* care and direction. (2) In Step Eleven, you were given the spiritual tools for seeking and obtaining His Will, His guidance, His power, and His peace at every turn. And growing in your understanding of each of these. So use them! In fact, it was common for Jack to say that the solution was: "God could and would if He were sought."

That is what our book is about.

We hardly need repeat here the very specific quiet time practices early AAs used. Nor need we discuss the high success rate (75%, 80%, 95%, 100%) they claimed. No one seemed to dispute those high success rate claims of the early days. Those claims were, in part, investigated and then confirmed, by John D. Rockefeller's agent, Frank Amos. And even today, people *still* admire the size and outreach of A.A., the numbers of people helped by it, and the availability of its resources. In large part, those resources are free for the taking. But increasingly, they are being dished out by people with little or no exposure to how the resources were used in the beginning to produce the early and highly successful recovery rate.

After his first five years of trying to help many many newcomers, the author began to utilize the historical tools of early A.A. with men he actually sponsored. He had endeavored to do so from the beginning; but he was intimidated within the rooms of A.A. and by the remarks of his first sponsor and his first support group. Gradually, he began to share *his* experience, not the experience of someone else. More and more boldly, he passed on the facts as to what early AAs did. Increasingly, the men he sponsored (and those the sponsees in turn attracted) became students of the Bible; participants in Bible fellowships; practitioners of Biblical ideas on prayer, guidance, healing, and deliverance; and bold witnesses to the power of God in their lives.

They took to heart and repeated the message: "God has done for me what I could not do for myself."

They stayed sober in percentages resembling those of early A.A. For the most part, they did not forsake A.A., but rather continued to serve *within* the A.A. Fellowship and to reach out to others with information on the Big Book, Twelve Steps, and spiritual growth. And the bottom line is: It worked!

What about Today?

Should AAs settle for any less today?

There is no barrier in today's A.A. to (1) atheists, (2) agnostics, (3) skeptics, (4) critics, (5) Christians, (6) Moslems, (7) Hindus, (8) Jews, (9) Buddhists, (10) Mormons, or people of other religious and non-religious persuasions. A.A. newcomers are free to pursue sobriety in whatever way they choose. But the author believes A.A. (as a Society) has no desire, and certainly no authorized mission, to establish some "universal religion" acceptable to all—believers and unbelievers alike. To those who turn up their noses at words which suggest that A.A. is "religious," it is appropriate here to quote the much-sought-after views of Dr. Harry Emerson Fosdick. In his 1939 book review of *Alcoholics Anonymous* (A.A.'s Big Book), Fosdick said, "The core of their whole procedure is religious."[66] Underscoring the importance to the Fellowship of Fosdick's endorsement, A.A.'s Conference-Approved literature quoted the foregoing, stated "Dr. Fosdick Again Recommends Us," and incorporated the following from Fosdick's autobiography: "Moreover, these testimonies bear witness to religion's reality, for Alcoholics Anonymous is deeply religious. . . . Roman Catholics, Jews, all kinds of Protestants, and even agnostics get together harmoniously on a religious basis."[67]

---

[66] *Alcoholics Anonymous Comes of Age: A Brief History of A.A.* (New York: Alcoholics Anonymous World Services, 1957), p. 323.

[67] *Alcoholics Anonymous Comes of Age*, pp. 323-24.

The author believes A.A. very much needs today to report truthfully, fully, and accurately exactly what the power and guidance of God meant in its earliest days. Prayer, listening, Bible study, and extensive religious reading were vital, observable, and well-accepted realities. And may AAs never forget Dr. Bob's bold, loving, and priceless words at the end of his story in the Big Book:

> If you think you are an atheist, an agnostic, a skeptic, or have any other form of intellectual pride which keeps you from accepting what is in this book, I feel sorry for you. If you still think you are strong enough to beat the game alone, that is your affair. But if you really and truly want to quit drinking liquor for good and all, and sincerely feel that you must have some help, we know that we have an answer for you. It never fails, if you go about it with one half the zeal you have been in the habit of showing when you were getting another drink. Your Heavenly Father will never let you down (p. 181)!

What was the answer of which Dr. Bob was speaking?

It was, of course, that "Your Heavenly Father will never let you down." Quiet Time, prayer, the Morning Watch, and meditation (meditation on the Bible and spiritual books) were the tickets to early A.A.'s information booth on exactly what God can do, how to seek His power, and how to gain deliverance from the Four Horsemen of which Bill Wilson wrote. Deliverance through these time-honored practices is as available today as it was in the A.A. of the 1930's. It worked then, and it will work now.

As Hebrews 11:6 states:

> But without faith, *it is* impossible to please *him* [God]: for he that cometh to God must believe that he is, and *that* he is a rewarder of them that diligently seek him.

END

Bibliography

Alcoholics Anonymous

Publications About

A Guide to the Twelve Steps of Alcoholics Anonymous. Akron: A.A. of Akron, n.d.

A Program for You: A Guide to the Big Book's Design for Living. Minnesota: Hazelden, 1991.

Alcoholics Anonymous. (multilith volume). New Jersey: Works Publishing Co., 1939.

A Manual for Alcoholics Anonymous. Akron: A.A. of Akron, n.d.

B., Dick. *Anne Smith's Journal, 1933-1939: A.A.'s Principles of Success.* 2d ed. Kihei, HI: Paradise Research Publications, Inc., 1996.

———. *Dr. Bob's Library: Books for Twelve Step Growth.* Kihei, HI: Paradise Research Publications, Inc., 1996.

———. *Hope: The Story of Geraldine D., Alina Lodge & Recovery.* Kihei, HI: Tincture of Time Press: 1997.

———. *New Light on Alcoholism: The A.A. Legacy from Sam Shoemaker.* Corte Madera, CA: Good Book Publishing Company, 1994.

———. *That Amazing Grace: The Mission and Message of A.A.'s Clarence and Grace S.* San Rafael, CA: Paradise Research Publications, 1996.

———. *The Akron Genesis of Alcoholics Anonymous.* Newton Edition. Paradise Researc Publications, Inc., 1998.

———. *The Books Early AAs Read for Spiritual Growth.* 6th ed. Kihei, HI: Paradise Research Publications, Inc., 1998.

———. *The Good Book and The Big Book: A.A.'s Roots in the Bible.* Bridge Builders Edition. Kihei, HI: Paradise Research Publications, Inc., 1997.

———. *The Oxford Group & Alcoholics Anonymous: A Design for Living That Works.* Kihei, HI: Paradise Research Publications, Inc., 1998.

———. *Turning Point: A History of Early A.A.'s Spiritual Roots and Successes.* Kihei, HI: Paradise Research Publications, Inc., 1997.

———. *Utilizing Early A.A.'s Spiritual Roots for Recovery Today.* Kihei, HI: Paradise Research Publications, Inc., 1998.

———, and Bill Pittman. *Courage to Change: The Christian Roots of the 12-Step Movement.* Grand Rapids, MI: Fleming H. Revell, 1994.

B., Jim. *Evolution of Alcoholics Anonymous.* New York: A.A. Archives.

B. Mel. *New Wine: The Spiritual Roots of the Twelve Step Miracle.* Minnesota: Hazelden, 1991.

Bishop, Charles, Jr. *The Washingtonians & Alcoholics Anonymous*. WV: The Bishop of Books, 1992.

———, and Bill Pittman. *To Be Continued . . . . . The Alcoholics Anonymous World Bibliography: 1935-1994*. Wheeling W. VA: The Bishop of Books, 1994.

Central Bulletin, Volumes I-II. Cleveland: Central Committee, Oct. 1942-Sept. 1944.

Conrad, Barnaby. *Time Is All We Have*. New York: Dell Publishing, 1986.

E., Bob. *Handwritten note to Lois Wilson on pamphlet entitled "Four Absolutes."* (copy made available to the author at Founders Day Archives Room in Akron, Ohio, in June, 1991).

———. Letter from Bob E. to Nell Wing. Stepping Stones Archives.

Fitzgerald, Robert. *The Soul of Sponsorship: The Friendship of Fr. Ed Dowling, S.J., and Bill Wilson in Letters*. Center City, MN: Hazelden, 1995.

Hunter, Willard, with assistance from M. D. B. *A.A.'s Roots in the Oxford Group*. New York: A.A. Archives, 1988.

Knippel, Charles T. *Samuel M. Shoemaker's Theological Influence on William G. Wilson's Twelve Step Spiritual Program of Recovery*. Ph. D. dissertation. St. Louis University, 1987.

Kurtz, Ernest. *Not-God: A History of Alcoholics Anonymous*. Exp. ed. Minnesota: Hazelden, 1991.

———. *Shame and Guilt: Characteristics of the Dependency Cycle*. Minnesota: Hazelden, 1981.

———, and Katherine Ketcham. *The Spirituality of Imperfection: Modern Wisdom from Classic Stories*. New York: Bantam Books, 1992.

McQ, Joe. *The Steps We Took*. Arkansas: August House Publishing, 1990.

Morreim, Dennis C. *Changed Lives: The Story of Alcoholics Anonymous*. Minneapolis: Augsburg Fortress, 1991.

Morse, Robert M, M.D., and Daniel K. Flavin, M.D. "The Definition of Alcoholism." *The Journal of the American Medical Association*. August 26, 1992, pp. 1012-14.

P., Wally. *But, for the Grace of God . . .: How Intergroups & Central Offices Carried the Message of Alcoholics Anonymous in the 1940s*. West Virginia: The Bishop of Books, 1995.

Poe, Stephen E. and Frances E. *A Concordance to Alcoholics Anonymous*. Nevada: Purple Salamander Press, 1990.

Playfair, William L., M.D. *The Useful Lie*. Illinois: Crossway Books, 1991.

Robertson, Nan. *Getting Better Inside Alcoholics Anonymous*. New York: William Morrow & Co., 1988.

S., Clarence. *Going through the Steps*. Winter Park, FL: Dick Stultz, 1981.

———. *Going through the Steps*. 2d ed. Altamonte Springs, FL: Stephen Foreman, 1985.

———. *My Higher Power—The Lightbulb*. Winter Park, FL: Dick Stultz, 1981.

———. *My Higher Power—The Lightbulb*. 2d ed. Altamonte Springs, FL: Stephen Foreman, 1985.

Second Reader for Alcoholics Anonymous. Akron: A.A. of Akron, n.d.

Seiberling, John F. *Origins of Alcoholics Anonymous*. (A transcript of remarks by Henrietta B. Seiberling: transcript prepared by Congressman John F. Seiberling of a telephone conversation with his mother, Henrietta in the spring of 1971): Employee Assistance Quarterly. 1985; (1); pp. 8-12.

Smith, Bob and Sue Smith Windows. *Children of the Healer*. Illinois: Parkside Publishing Corporation, 1992.

Spiritual Milestones in Alcoholics Anonymous. Akron: A.A. of Akron, n.d.

T., John. *A.A.: God's Instrument*. Reprint of speech delivered at Fourth Anniversary Meeting of the Chicago A.A. Group on October 5, 1943.

The Four Absolutes. Cleveland: Cleveland Central Committee of A.A., n. d.

Thomsen, Robert. *Bill W*. New York: Harper & Row, 1975.

Wilson, Bill. *How The Big Book Was Put Together*. New York: A.A. General Services Archives, Transcript of Bill Wilson Speech delivered in Fort Worth, Texas, 1954.

————. *Bill Wilson's Original Story*. Bedford Hills, New York: Stepping Stones Archives, n.d., a manuscript whose individual lines are numbered 1 to 1180.

————. "Main Events: Alcoholics Anonymous Fact Sheet by Bill." November 1, 1954. Stepping Stones Archives. Bedford Hills, New York.

————. "The Fellowship of Alcoholics Anonymous." *Quarterly Journal of Studies on Alcohol*. Yale University, 1945, pp. 461-73.

————. *W. G. Wilson Recollections*. Bedford Hills, New York: Stepping Stones Archives, September 1, 1954 transcript of Bill's dictations to Ed B.

Wilson, Jan R., and Judith A. Wilson. *Addictionary: A Primer of Recovery Terms and Concepts from Abstinence to Withdrawal*. New York: Simon and Schuster, 1992.

Wilson, Lois. *Lois Remembers*. New York: Al-Anon Family Group Headquarters, 1987.

Windows, Sue Smith. (daughter of A.A.'s Co-Founder, Dr. Bob). Typewritten Memorandum entitled, *Henrietta and early Oxford Group Friends, by Sue Smith Windows*. Delivered to the author of this book by Sue Smith Windows at Akron, June, 1991.

Wing, Nell. *Grateful to Have Been There: My 42 Years with Bill and Lois, and the Evolution of Alcoholics Anonymous*. Illinois: Parkside Publishing Corporation, 1992.

Publications Approved by Alcoholics Anonymous

Alcoholics Anonymous. 3rd ed. New York: Alcoholics Anonymous World Services, Inc., 1976.

Alcoholics Anonymous. 1st ed. New Jersey: Works Publishing, 1939.

Alcoholics Anonymous Comes of Age. New York: Alcoholics Anonymous World Services, Inc., 1957.

A Newcomer Asks . . . York, England: A.A. Sterling Area Services, n.d.

As Bill Sees It: The A.A. Way of Life . . . *selected writings of A.A.'s Co-Founder*. New York: Alcoholics Anonymous World Services, Inc., 1967.

Daily Reflections. New York: Alcoholics Anonymous World Services, Inc., 1991.

DR. BOB and the Good Oldtimers. New York: Alcoholics Anonymous World Services, Inc., 1980.

44 Questions. New York: Works Publishing, Inc., 1952.

Members of the Clergy Ask about Alcoholics Anonymous. New York: Alcoholics Anonymous World Services, 1961, 1979-revised 1992, according to 1989 Conference Advisory Action.

Pass It On. New York: Alcoholics Anonymous World Services, Inc., 1984.

Questions & Answers on Sponsorship. New York: Alcoholics Anonymous World Services, Inc., 1976.

The A.A. Grapevine: "RHS"—issue dedicated to the memory of the Co-Founder of Alcoholics Anonymous, DR. BOB. New York: A.A. Grapevine, Inc., 1951.

The Co-Founders of Alcoholics Anonymous. New York: Alcoholics Anonymous World Services, Inc., 1972.

The Language of the Heart. Bill W.'s Grapevine Writings. New York: The A.A. Grapevine, Inc., 1988.

This is A.A. . . . An Introduction to the AA Recovery Program. New York: Alcoholics Anonymous World Services, Inc., 1984.

Twelve Steps and Twelve Traditions. New York: Alcoholics Anonymous World Services, Inc., 1953.

The Bible—Versions of and Books About

Authorized King James Version. New York: Thomas Nelson, 1984.

Bullinger, Ethelbert W. *A Critical Lexicon and Concordance to the English and Greek New Testament.* Michigan: Zondervan, 1981.

Burns, Kenneth Charles. "The Rhetoric of Christology." Master's thesis, San Francisco State University, 1991.

Every Catholic's Guide to the Sacred Scriptures. Nashville: Thomas Nelson, 1990.

Harnack, Adolph. *The Expansion of Christianity in the First Three Centuries.* New York: G. P. Putnam's Sons, Volume I, 1904; Volume II, 1905.

Jukes, Andrew. *The Names of GOD in Holy Scripture.* Michigan: Kregel Publications, 1967.

Megivern, James J. *Official Catholic Teachings: Bible Interpretation.* North Carolina: McGrath Publishing Company, 1978.

Mau, Charles P. *James M. Gray As a Christian Educator.* Master's thesis. Fuller Theological Seminary, 1963.

Moffatt, James. *A New Translation of the Bible.* New York: Harper & Brothers, 1954.

New Bible Dictionary. 2d ed. Wheaton, Illinois: Tyndale House Publishers, 1987.

On, J. Edwin. *Full Surrender.* London: Marshall, Morgan & Scott, 1951.

Phillips, J. B. *The New Testament in Modern English.* New York: The Macmillan Company, 1958.

Puskas, Charles B. *An Introduction to the New Testament.* Mass.: Hendrickson Publishers, 1989.

Recovery Devotional Bible: New International Version. Grand Rapids, MI: Zondervan, 1993.

Revised Standard Version. New York: Thomas Nelson, 1952.

Schaff, Philip. *History of the Christian Church.* Grand Rapids, MI: Eerdmans, Volume II, 1956.

Serenity: A Companion for Twelve Step Recovery. Nashville: Thomas Nelson, 1990.

Strong, James. *The Exhaustive Concordance of the Bible.* Iowa: Riverside Book and Bible House, n.d.

The Abingdon Bible Commentary. New York: Abingdon Press, 1929.

The Companion Bible. Grand Rapids, MI: Kregel Publications, 1990.

The Life Recovery Bible: The Living Bible. Wheaton, IL: Tyndale House, 1992.

The Revised English Bible. Oxford: Oxford University Press, 1989.

Vine, W. E. *Vine's Expository Dictionary of Old and New Testament Words*. New York: Fleming H. Revell, 1981.

Young's Analytical Concordance to the Bible. New York: Thomas Nelson, 1982.

Zodhiates, Spiros. *The Hebrew-Greek Key Study Bible*. 6th ed. AMG Publishers, 1991.

Bible Devotionals

Chambers, Oswald. *My Utmost for His Highest*. London: Simpkin Marshall, Ltd., 1927.

Clark, Glenn, *I Will Lift Up Mine Eyes*. New York: Harper & Brothers, 1937.

Fosdick, Harry Emerson. *The Meaning of Prayer*. New York: Association Press, 1915.

Holm, Nora Smith. *The Runner's Bible*. New York: Houghton Mifflin Company, 1915.

Jones, E. Stanley. *Abundant Living*. New York: Abingdon-Cokesbury Press, 1942.

―――. *Victorious Living*. New York: Abingdon Press, 1936.

The Upper Room: Daily Devotions for Family and Individual Use. Quarterly. 1st issue: April, May, June, 1935. Edited by Grover Carlton Emmons. Nashville: General Committee on Evangelism through the Department of Home Missions, Evangelism, Hospitals, Board of Missions, Methodist Episcopal Church, South.

Tileston, Mary W. *Daily Strength for Daily Needs*. Boston: Roberts Brothers, 1893.

Publications by or about the Oxford Group & Oxford Group People

Allen, Geoffrey Francis. *He That Cometh*. New York: The Macmillan Company, 1933.

Almond, Harry J. *Foundations for Faith*. 2d ed. London: Grosvenor Books, 1980.

Begbie, Harold. *Life Changers*. New York: G. P. Putnam's Sons, 1927.

Belden, Kenneth D. *Beyond the Satellites: If God Is Speaking-Are We Listening?* London: Grosvenor Books, 1987.

―――. *Meeting Moral Re-Armament*. London: Grosvenor Books, 1979.

―――. *Reflections on Moral Re-Armament*. London: Grosvenor Books, 1983.

―――. *The Hour of the Helicopter*. Somerset, England: Linden Hall, 1992.

Benson, Clarence Irving. *The Eight Points of the Oxford Group*. London: Humphrey Milford, Oxford University Press, 1936.

Blake, Howard C. *Way to Go: Adventures in Search of God's Will*. Burbank, CA: Pooh Stix Press, 1992.

Brown, Philip Marshall. *The Venture of Belief*. New York: Fleming H. Revell, 1935.

Buchman, Frank N. D. *Remaking the World*. London: Blandford Press, 1961.

―――, and Sherwood Eddy. *Ten Suggestions for Personal Work* (not located).

―――. *The Revolutionary Path: Moral Re-Armament in the thinking of Frank Buchman*. London: Grosvenor, 1975.

Cook, Sydney and Garth Lean. *The Black and White Book: A Handbook of Revolution*. London: Blandford Press, 1972.

Day, Sherwood Sunderland. *The Principles of the Group*. Oxford: University Press, n.d.

Dorsey, Theodore H. *From a Far Country: The Conversion Story of a Campaigner for Christ*. Huntington, Indiana: Our Sunday Visitor Press, n.d.

Foot, Stephen. *Life Began Yesterday*. New York: Harper & Brothers, 1935.

Forde, Eleanor Napier. *The Guidance of God*. London: The Oxford Group, 1927.

Hadden, Richard M. "Christ's Program for World-Reconstruction: Studies in the Sermon on the Mount." *The Calvary Evangel*, 1934-35, pp. 11-14, 44-49, 73-77, 104-07, 133-36.

Harris, Irving. *An Outline of the Life of Christ*. New York: The Oxford Group, 1935.

———. *Out in Front: Forerunners of Christ. A Study of the Lives of Eight Great Men*. New York: The Calvary Evangel, 1942.

———. *The Breeze of the Spirit*. New York: The Seabury Press, 1978.

Hicks, Roger. *How Augustine Found Faith: Told in his own words from F. J. Sheed's translation of The Confessions of St.   Augustine*. N.p., 1956.

———. *How to Read the Bible*. London: Moral Re-Armament, 1940.

———. *The Lord's Prayer and Modern Man*. London: Blandford Press, 1967.

Hofmeyr, Bremer. *How to Change*. New York: Moral Re-Armament, n.d.

———. *How to Listen*. London: The Oxford Group, 1941.

Howard, Peter. *Frank Buchman's Secret*. Garden City: New York: Doubleday & Company, Inc., 1961.

———. *That Man Frank Buchman*. London: Blandford Press, 1946.

———. *The World Rebuilt*. New York. Duell, Sloan & Pearce, 1951.

Hunter, T. Willard, with assistance from M.D.B. *A.A.'s Roots in the Oxford Group*. New York: A.A. Archives, 1988.

———. *"It Started Right There" Behind the Twelve Steps and the Self-help Movement*. Oregon: Grosvenor Books, 1994.

———. *World Changing Through Life Changing*. Thesis, Newton Center, Mass: Andover-Newton Theological School, 1977.

Hutchinson, Michael. *A Christian Approach to Other Faiths*. London: Grosvenor Books, 1991.

———. *The Confessions*. (privately published study of St. Augustine's *Confessions*).

Jones, Olive M. *Inspired Children*. New York: Harper & Brothers, 1933.

———. *Inspired Youth*. New York: Harper & Brothers, 1938.

Kitchen, V. C. *I Was a Pagan*. New York: Harper & Brothers, 1934.

Lean, Garth. *Cast Out Your Nets*. London: Grosvenor, 1990.

———. *Frank Buchman: A Life*. London: Constable, 1985.

———. *Good God, It Works*. London: Blandford Press, 1974.

———. *On the Tail of a Comet: The Life of Frank Buchman*. Colorado Springs: Helmers & Howard, 1988.

———, and Morris Martin. *New Leadership*. London: William Heinemann, 1936.

Leon, Philip. *The Philosophy of Courage or the Oxford Group Way*. New York: Oxford University Press, 1939.

Macmillan, Ebenezer. *Seeking and Finding*. New York: Harper & Brothers, 1933.

Martin, Morris H. *The Thunder and the Sunshine*. Washington D.C.: MRA, n.d.

——. *Born to Live in the Future*. n.l.: Up With People, 1991.

Mowat, R. C. *Modern Prophetic Voices: From Kierkegaard to Buchman*. Oxford: New Cherwel Press, 1994.

———. *The Message of Frank Buchman*. London: Blandford Press, n.d.

———. *Decline and Renewal: Europe Ancient and Modern*. Oxford: New Cherwel Press, 1991.

Newton, Eleanor Forde. *I Always Wanted Adventure*. London: Grosvenor, 1992.

Newton, James Draper. *Uncommon Friends: Life with Thomas Edison, Henry Ford, Harvey Firestone, Alexis Carrel, & Charles Lindbergh*. New York: Harcourt Brace, 1987.

Nichols, Beverley. *The Fool Hath Said*. Garden City: Doubleday, Doran & Company, 1936.

Phillimore, Miles. *Just for Today*. Privately published pamphlet, 1940.

Reynolds, Amelia S. *New Lives for Old*. New York. Fleming H. Revell, 1929.

Rose, Cecil. *When Man Listens*. New York: Oxford University Press, 1937.

Rose, Howard J. *The Quiet Time*. New York: Oxford Group at 61 Gramercy Park, North, 1937.

Russell, Arthur J. *For Sinners Only*. London: Hodder & Stoughton, 1932.

Sangster, W. E. *God Does Guide Us*. New York: The Abingdon Press, 1934.

Spoerri, Theophil. *Dynamic out of Silence: Frank Buchman's Relevance Today*. Translated by John Morrison. London: Grosvenor Books, 1976.

Streeter, Burnett Hillman. *The God Who Speaks*. London: Macmillan & Co., Ltd., 1936.

The Layman with a Notebook. *What Is the Oxford Group?* London: Oxford University Press, 1933.

Thornton-Duesbury, Julian P. *Sharing*. The Oxford Group. n.d.

Viney, Hallen. *How Do I Begin?* The Oxford Group, 61 Gramercy Park, New York., 1937.

Waddy, Charis. *The Skills of Discernment*. London: Grosvenor Books, 1977.

Walter, Howard A. *Soul Surgery: Some Thoughts On Incisive Personal Work*. Oxford: The Oxford Group, 1928.

Weatherhead, Leslie D. *Discipleship*. London: Student Christian Movement Press, 1934.

———. *How Can I Find God?* London: Fleming H. Revell, 1934.

———. *Psychology and Life*. New York: Abingdon Press, 1935.

Winslow, Jack C. *Church in Action* (no data available to author).

———. *Vital Touch with God: How to Carry on Adequate Devotional Life*. The Evangel, 8 East 40th St., New York, n.d.

———. *When I Awake*. London: Hodder & Stoughton, 1938.

———. *Why I Believe in the Oxford Group*. London: Hodder & Stoughton, 1934.

Books by or about Oxford Group Mentors

Bushnell, Horace. *The New Life*. London: Strahan & Co., 1868.

Chapman, J. Wilbur. *Life and Work of Dwight L. Moody*. Philadelphia, 1900.

Cheney, Mary B. *Life and Letters of Horace Bushnell*. New York: Harper & Brothers, 1890.

Drummond, Henry. *Essays and Addresses*. New York: James Potts & Company, 1904.

———. *Natural Law in the Spiritual World*. Potts Edition.

———. *The Changed Life*. New York: James Potts & Company, 1891.

———. *The Greatest Thing in the World and Other Addresses*. London: Collins, 1953.

———. *The Ideal Life*. London: Hodder & Stoughton, 1897.

———. *The New Evangelism and Other Papers*. London: Hodder & Stoughton, 1899.

Edwards, Robert L. *Of Singular Genius, of Singular Grace: A Biography of Horace Bushnell.* Cleveland: The Pilgrim Press, 1992.

Findlay, James F., Jr. *Dwight L. Moody American Evangelist.* Chicago, University of Chicago Press, 1969.

Fitt, Emma Moody, *Day by Day with D. L. Moody.* Chicago: Moody Press, n.d.

Goodspeed, Edgar J. *The Wonderful Career of Moody and Sankey in Great Britain and America.* New York: Henry S. Goodspeed & Co., 1876.

Guldseth, Mark O. *Streams.* Alaska: Fritz Creek Studios, 1982.

Hopkins, C. Howard. *John R. Mott, a Biography.* Grand Rapids: William B. Erdmans Publishing Company, 1979.

James, William. *The Varieties of Religious Experience.* New York: First Vintage Books/The Library of America, 1990.

Meyer, F. B. *Five Musts.* Chicago: Moody Press, 1927.

————.*The Secret of Guidance.* New York: Fleming H. Revell, 1896.

Moody, Paul D. *My Father: An Intimate Portrait of Dwight Moody.* Boston: Little Brown, 1938.

Moody, William R. *The Life of D. L. Moody.* New York: Fleming H. Revell, 1900.

Mott, John R. *The Evangelization of the World in This Generation.* London, 1901.

————. *Addresses and Papers* (no further data at this time).

————. *Five Decades and a Forward View.* 4th ed. New York: Harper & Brothers, 1939.

Pollock, J. C. *Moody: A Biographical Portrait of the Pacesetter in Modern Mass Evangelism.* New York: Macmillan, 1963.

Smith, George Adam. *The Life of Henry Drummond.* New York: McClure, Phillips & Co., 1901.

Speer, Robert E. *Studies of the Man Christ Jesus.* New York: Fleming H. Revell, 1896.

————. *The Marks of a Man.* New York: Hodder & Stoughton, 1907.

————. *The Principles of Jesus.* New York: Fleming H. Revell Company, 1902.

Stewart, George, Jr. *Life of Henry B. Wright.* New York: Association Press, 1925.

Wright, Henry B. *The Will of God and a Man's Lifework.* New York: The Young Men's Christian Association Press, 1909.

Publications by or about Samuel Moor Shoemaker, Jr.

Shoemaker, Samuel Moor, Jr. "A 'Christian Program.'" In *Groups That Work: The Key to Renewal . . . for Churches, Communities, and Individuals.* Compiled by Walden Howard and the Editors of *Faith At Work.* Michigan: Zondervan, 1967.

————. "Act As If." *Christian Herald.* October, 1954.

————. "A First Century Christian Fellowship: A Defense of So-called Buchmanism by One of Its Leaders." Reprinted from *The Churchman,* circa 1928.

————. *A Young Man's View of the Ministry.* New York: Association Press, 1923.

————. *Calvary Church Yesterday and Today.* New York: Fleming H. Revell, 1936.

————. *Calvary Mission.* Pamphlet. N.d.

————. *Children of the Second Birth.* New York: Fleming H. Revell, 1927.

————. *Christ's Words from the Cross.* New York: Fleming H. Revell, 1933.

————. *Confident Faith.* New York: Fleming H. Revell, 1932.

———. "Creative Relationships." In *Together*. New York: Abingdon Cokesbury Press, 1946.

———. *Faith at Work*. A symposium edited by Samuel Moor Shoemaker. Hawthorne Books, 1958.

———. *God's Control*. New York: Fleming H. Revell, 1939.

———. *How to Become a Christian*. New York: Harper & Brothers, 1953.

———. *How You Can Help Other People*. New York: E. P. Dutton & Co., 1946.

———. "How to Find God." *The Calvary Evangel*. July, 1957, pp. 1-24.

———. *If I Be Lifted Up*. New York: Fleming H. Revell, 1931.

———. *Morning Radio Talk No. 1, by Reverend Samuel M. Shoemaker*, American Broadcasting Co., 1 page transcript of program for October 4, 1945.

———. *My Life-Work and My Will*. Pamphlet. Circa 1930.

———. *National Awakening*. New York: Harper & Brothers, 1936.

———. *One Boy's Influence*. New York: Association Press, 1925.

———. *Realizing Religion*. New York: Association Press, 1923.

———. *Religion That Works*. New York: Fleming H. Revell, 1928.

———. *Sam Shoemaker at His Best*. New York: Faith At Work, 1964.

———. *So I Stand by the Door and Other Verses*. Pittsburgh: n.p., 1958.

———. *The Calvary Evangel, monthly articles in*. New York. Calvary Episcopal Church.

———. *The Church Can Save the World*. New York: Harper & Brothers, 1938.

———. *The Conversion of the Church*. New York: Fleming H. Revell, 1932.

———. *The Gospel According to You*. New York: Fleming H. Revell, 1934.

———. "The Spiritual Angle." *The A.A. Grapevine*. New York: The A.A. Grapevine, Inc., October, 1955.

———. "The Spiritual Part of AA." *The A.A. Grapevine*. November, 1960.

———. "The Way to Find God." *The Calvary Evangel*. August, 1935.

———. "Those Twelve Steps As I Understand Them." *Best of the Grapevine: Volume II*. New York: The A.A. Grapevine, Inc., 1986.

———. "Transcript of Reverend Samuel M. Shoemaker talk to Third International A.A. Convention, 25th A.A. Anniversary." [Sunday, July 3, 1960, 11:00 AM, Memorial Stadium, Long Beach, CA].

———. *Twice-Born Ministers*. New York: Fleming H. Revell, 1929.

———. *What the Church Has to Learn from Alcoholics Anonymous*. Reprint of 1956 sermon. Available at A.A. Archives, New York.

———. *With the Holy Spirit and with Fire*. New York: Harper & Brothers, 1960.

Cuyler, John Potter, Jr. *Calvary Church in Action*. New York: Fleming H. Revell, 1934.

Harris, Irving. *The Breeze of the Spirit*. New York: The Seabury Press, 1978.

Norton-Taylor, Duncan. "Businessmen on Their Knees." *Fortune*. October, 1953.

Olsson, Karl A. "The History of Faith at Work" (five parts). *Faith at Work News*. 1982-1983.

"Pittsburgh Man of the Year." *Pittsburgh Post Gazette*. January 12, 1956.

"Sam Shoemaker and Faith at Work." Pamphlet on file at Faith At Work, Inc., 150 S. Washington St., Suite 204, Falls Church, VA 22046.

Sider, Michael J. *Taking the Gospel to the Point: Evangelicals in Pittsburgh and the Origins of the Pittsburgh Leadership Foundation*. Pittsburgh: Pittsburgh Leadership Foundation, n.d.

"Ten of the Greatest American Preachers." *Newsweek*. March 28, 1955.

The Pittsburgh Experiment's Groups. Pittsburgh: The Pittsburgh Experiment, n.d.

Tools for Christian Living. Pittsburgh: The Pittsburgh Experiment, n.d.

Spiritual Literature-Non-Oxford Group

[Almost all of these books were owned, studied, recommended, and loaned to others by Dr. Bob and his wife, Anne.]

Allen, James. *As a Man Thinketh*. New York: Peter Pauper Press, n.d.

Brother Lawrence. *The Practice of the Presence of God*. Pennsylvania: Whitaker House, 1982.

Carruthers, Donald W. *How to Find Reality in Your Morning Devotions*. Pennsylvania: State College, n.d.

Chambers, Oswald. *Studies in the Sermon on the Mount*. London: Simpkin, Marshall, Ltd., n.d.

Clark, Glenn. *Fishers of Men*. Boston: Little, Brown, 1928.

———. *I Will Lift Up Mine Eyes*. New York: Harper & Brothers, 1937.

———. *The Lord's Prayer and Other Talks on Prayer from The Camps Farthest Out*. Minnesota: Macalester Publishing Co., 1932.

———. *The Soul's Sincere Desire*. Boston: Little, Brown, 1925.

———. *Touchdowns for the Lord. The Story of "Dad" A. J. Elliott*. Minnesota: Macalester Park Publishing Co., 1947.

Fosdick, Harry Emerson. *As I See Religion*. New York: Grosset & Dunlap, 1932.

———. *The Man from Nazareth*. New York: Harper & Brothers, 1949.

———. *The Meaning of Faith*. New York: The Abingdon Press, 1917.

———. *The Meaning of Prayer*. New York: Association Press, 1915.

———. *The Meaning of Service*. London: Student Christian Movement, 1921.

Fox, Emmet.*The Sermon on the Mount*. New York: Harper & Row, 1934.

———. Pamphlets: *Getting Results by Prayer* (1933); *The Great Adventure* (1937); *You Must Be Born Again* (1936).

Glover, T. R. *The Jesus of History*. New York: Association Press, 1930.

Gordon, S. D. *The Quiet Time*. London: Fleming, n.d.

Heard, Gerald. *A Preface to Prayer*. New York: Harper & Brothers, 1944.

Hickson, James Moore. *Heal the Sick*. London: Methuen & Co., 1925.

James, William. *The Varieties of Religious Experience*. New York: First Vintage Press/The Library of America Edition, 1990.

Jones, E. Stanley. *Abundant Living*. New York: Cokesbury Press, 1942.

———. *Along the Indian Road*. New York: Abingdon Press, 1939.

———. *Christ and Human Suffering*. New York: Abingdon Press, 1930.

———. *Christ at the Round Table*. New York: Abingdon Press, 1928.

———. *The Choice Before Us*. New York: Abingdon Press, 1937.

———. *The Christ of Every Road*. New York: Abingdon Press, 1930.

———. *The Christ of the Indian Road*. New York: Abingdon Press, 1925.

———. *The Christ of the Mount*. New York: Abingdon Press, 1930.

———. *Victorious Living*. New York: Abingdon Press, 1936.

Jung, Dr. Carl G. *Modern Man in Search of a Soul*. New York: Harcourt Brace Jovanovich, 1933.

Kagawa, Toyohiko. *Love: The Law of Life*. Philadelphia: The John C. Winston Company, 1929.

Kempis, Thomas à. *The Imitation of Christ*. Georgia: Mercer University Press, 1989.

Laubach, Frank. *Prayer (Mightiest Force in the World)*. New York: Fleming H. Revell, 1946.

Layman, Charles M. *A Primer of Prayer*. Nashville: Tidings, 1949.

Parker, William R., and Elaine St. Johns. *Prayer Can Change Your Life*. New ed. New York: Prentice Hall, 1957.

Rawson, F. L. *The Nature of True Prayer*. Chicago: The Marlowe Company, n.d.

Sheldon, Charles M. *In His Steps*. Nashville, Broadman Press, 1935.

Silkey, Charles Whitney. *Jesus and Our Generation*. Chicago: University of Chicago Press, 1925.

Speer, Robert E.. *Studies of the Man Christ Jesus*. New York: Fleming H. Revell, 1896.

Stalker, James. *The Life of Jesus Christ*. New York: Fleming H. Revell, 1891.

The Confessions of St. Augustine. Translated by E. B. Pusey. A Cardinal Edition. New York: Pocket Books, 1952.

Williams, R. Llewelen, *God's Great Plan, a Guide to the Bible*. Hoverhill Destiny Publishers, n.d.

Willitts, Ethel R. *Healing in Jesus Name*. Chicago: Ethel R. Willitts Evangelists, 1931.

Index

A

à Kempis, Thomas (*The Imitation of Christ*) 34
A.A. Archives 131, 132
AA of Akron 110
  A Manual for Alcoholics Anonymous 110, 131
Abandon yourself 76
Absolute honesty 85, 87
Absolute love 85, 87
Absolute purity 85, 87
Absolute unselfishness 85, 87
Acts 1:4 22, 60, 96
Acts 1:4, 5, 8 22
Acts 1:4-5, 8 60
Acts 1:8 95, 123
Acts 2:1-13 95
Acts 2:4 115
Acts 2:38 61
Acts 2:38-39 61
Acts 22:10 93, 105
Acts 4:7 115
Acts 4:9-10, 12 115
Acts 8 70, 71
Acts 8:26 71
Acts 8:26-35 71
Acts 9:3-20 13
Acts 9:6 30, 93, 105
Acts 10:43 61
Acts 10:43-44 61
Acts 14:15 110
Acts 17:11 69
Acts 19:1-6 54
Agnostics 129

Air (two-way prayer) 49, 88
Alcoholism
  100% hopeless, apart from divine help 109
Almond, Harry 22, 57, 69, 73, 89
Amends 5
Amos 8:11 94
Amos, Frank B. 6, 94, 128
Anxiety 48, 67, 95, 98, 105, 117
  take no thought for [be not anxious about]--Matt. 6:25-34 66, 105
  thou wilt keep him in perfect peace (Isa. 26:3) 93, 105
Art (Soul Surgery) 18, 23, 33, 61, 67
As Bill Sees It 3, 119
Atheist(s) 130
Attentive prayer 46
Awakening 53, 62, 103, 119, 127

B

B., Mel (A.A. member—see also *New Wine*) 125
Barrier(s) 49, 95, 129
Basic ideas (A.A.'s) 5, 73
Be still, and know that I am God 29, 66, 92, 105
Beatitudes 15
Begbie, Harold 100, 109
Belden, K. D. 18, 28, 37, 55, 56, 73
Beliefs 111, 125
Believer 28, 38, 112, 119

145

"your Father" 44, 95

God Who Speaks, The (B. H. Streeter) 11, 22, 28, 29, 44, 45, 53, 55, 60, 61, 91

God's guidance 1, 13, 57, 76, 84, 88, 89, 100, 101, 103, 104

God's plan 44, 45

God's will 12, 15, 37-39, 43, 46, 55, 65, 77, 84, 100, 111, 116, 117,
  general will 15, 68
  knowledge of 100
  particular will 12, 13, 111
  power to carry that out 4, 99, 100
  universal will 15, 16, 68, 70, 111

Good Book (the Bible) 2, 5, 9, 10, 14, 16, 19, 25, 32, 56, 58, 66, 67, 69, 72, 74, 75, 83, 99-102, 107, 109, 112, 119, 131

Gospels 20, 59

Grace 9, 15, 37, 55, 58, 85, 105, 108, 110, 115, 116, 131, 132

Greatest Thing in the World, The (Henry Drummond) 91, 113, 120

Group Of Drunks. *See* God; absurd names for 107

Guidance 1, 8, 10-13, 19, 25, 26, 29, 35, 38, 39, 42-51, 53, 57, 58, 59, 64, 65, 67, 69, 70, 74, 76, 80-84, 86, 88, 89, 90, 91, 97-105, 111, 112, 117, 118, 120, 128, 130
  be still, and know that I am God 29, 66, 92, 105
  Commit thy way unto the Lord 93
  For we walk by faith 93
  He shall direct thy paths 29, 93
  I will guide thee with mine eye 74, 93

Lord, what wilt thou have me to do 30, 93, 105

speak, Lord; for thy servant heareth 30, 92, 105

the wisdom that is from above 84

Guldseth, Mark O. (*Streams*) 92

H

Habakkuk 2:2 21, 31
Habakkuk 2:2-3 21
Hartford Theological Seminary 43
He That Cometh (Geoffrey Allen) 116, 130
Healing 110, 111, 114, 117, 118, 126, 128
Hebrews 10:31 110
Hebrews 11:6 130
Helpful books (Eleventh Step) 14, 65, 70, 71, 102, 105, 111, 112, 114
Hicks, Roger 27, 113
Higher power 107, 108, 132
Holm, Nora Smith (*The Runner's Bible*) 10, 21, 113
Holy Spirit 22, 35, 41, 46, 49, 51, 52, 59, 60, 64, 69-71, 79, 82, 83, 95, 96
Honesty 85, 87
Hope 2, 53, 61, 110, 131
Houck, James 89, 92
How Do I Begin? (Hallen Viney) 10, 11, 31, 78, 82, 87, 91
Howard, Peter (Frank Buchman's successor) 58
Hunter, T. Willard 43, 89, 132
Hutchinson, Michael 89, 92, 93

I

If any man willeth to do his will, he shall know 88
Imitation of Christ, The (Thomas à Kempis) 34

Inspiration 8, 22, 38, 42, 52, 82,
   103
Intercession 10, 52, 74, 75, 77,
   117
Intuitive thought 103, 104
Invented (nobody invented A.A.)
   3, 4
Inventory 5, 87, 102
Isaiah 1:1-2 21
Isaiah 1:4 48
Isaiah 11:2 13
Isaiah 26:3 66, 67, 93, 98, 105,
   119
Isaiah 26:3-4 98
Isaiah 40:18 109
Isaiah 50:4 9, 10, 18, 93
Isaiah 50:4-5 18
Isaiah 58:11 59
Isaiah 59:21 60
It works 4, 32

J

James 1:5 38, 74, 92
James 1:6 117
James 1:12-17 98
James 1:17 83, 118
James 1:21-22 27
James 2:14-18 98
James 3:14-17 85
James 5:15 75, 102
James 5:15-16 75
James 5:16 32
Jeremiah 1:2-4 21
Jeremiah 7:23 12, 93
Jeremiah 30:2 10, 31, 92
Jesus Christ 15, 19-22, 25, 30, 31,
   34, 44-47, 51, 53-55, 57-62,
   65, 67, 71, 72, 74, 78,
   83-85, 97, 98, 103, 106,
   112, 113, 115, 117, 122,
   123
  Redeemer 29
  Savior 55, 115
  Teacher 2, 38, 49, 113

Job 6:8 40
John 10:10 99, 117, 119
John 14:6 115
John 14:13-14 117
John 14:16, 26 22
John 14:26 93
John 16:13 79
John 16:13-14 79
John 16:15 79
John 16:23-24, 26 117
John 17:14 20
John 17:17 20
Jones, E. Stanley 22, 27, 30, 31,
   71, 92, 113
  The Christ of the Mount 113
  Victorious Living 22, 25-27,
   30, 31, 92, 120
Jude 19 59
Judges 7:19 16
Jukes, Andrew (*The Names of God
   in Scripture*) 109

K

Kagawa, Toyohiko 113
Kindergarten
  spiritual (A.A.) 112, 119
Kindness 18
Kingdom of God 54, 106, 115
Kitchen, Victor C. 100, 104
Knippel, Charles T. (*S. M.
   Shoemaker's Theological,*
   etc.) 132
Kurtz, Ernest (*Not God: A History
   of Alcoholics Anonymous*)
   63, 70, 120, 125, 132

L

Lamentations 2:19 16, 17, 28
Layman with a Notebook, the
   (*What Is The Oxford
   Group?*) 83, 91, 106
Leading thoughts 13

O

Obedience 11, 42, 88
Obeys, when man 11, 89
Oxford Group, the 4-6, 8-15, 19,
    26-29, 31, 33, 34, 35, 38,
    41, 43, 45-47, 49, 53,
    55-59, 61, 64, 67-70, 72,
    73, 76, 78, 79, 80-90,
    89-94, 99-106, 111-115,
    120-122, 131-132
  alcoholic squad of 14, 56, 90
  businessmen's team 104, 113
  founder 11, 45, 57, 80
  house party (-ies) 86, 113
  meetings 86, 89, 90, 89, 90
  team(s) 26, 89, 104, 113

P

Path 29, 38, 93
Patience 28, 102, 110
Peace
  thou wilt keep him in perfect
    peace (Isa. 26:3) 93, 105
Philippians 4:6-7 31, 67, 74, 98,
    106, 117
Philippians 4:19 98
Phillimore, Miles 69, 73, 118
Pittman, Bill (*AA The Way It
    Began*) 2, 131, 132
Plan (God's) 37, 44, 45, 48, 72,
    76, 80, 100, 104
Power 4, 14, 16, 18, 25, 37, 46,
    47, 50, 54, 55, 60, 70, 85,
    94, 95, 96, 99-101, 107-110,
    114-116, 118, 121, 122,
    123, 126, 128, 130, 132
  a stronger, than his 54, 123
  filled with the Holy Ghost (Acts
    4:31, 33) 115
  from on high 60, 115
  if any man be in Christ (2 Cor.
    5:17) 55

ye shall receive (Acts 1:8) 60,
    95, 123
Pray, how to 73, 113
Prayer 1, 3-10, 16-18, 23, 24, 27,
    29-32, 35-40, 43, 46, 47,
    49-52, 57, 58, 62-70, 72,
    73, 75, 77, 79, 81, 83, 87,
    90, 92, 93, 96, 99, 100,
    102, 103-106, 110, 111,
    113, 114, 116-121, 126,
    128, 13
  adoration 74, 117
  intercession 10, 52, 74, 75, 77,
    117
  petition 10, 40, 52, 65, 75, 77
  thanksgiving 10, 30, 31, 52,
    66, 74, 75, 77, 106, 117
Pride 130
Principles of the Group, The
    (Sherwood S. Day) 6
Progress 47
Prophets 11, 34, 51, 71, 94
Protestant 12, 26, 126
Proverbs 1:3 21
Proverbs 3:5 29, 99, 118
Proverbs 3:6 93
Psalm 1:2-3 24
Psalm 5:1-3 9, 27
Psalm 5:3 10, 18, 65, 92
Psalm 5:3-5 18
Psalm 19:14 29
Psalm 23 110
Psalm 32:8 74, 93, 118
Psalm 34:4 117
Psalm 37:5 93
Psalm 37:7 10, 28, 40, 68, 78
Psalm 46:10 29, 66, 67, 92, 105
Psalm 50:14-15 30
Psalm 59:16 18
Psalm 62:5 29, 40
Psalm 62:5-8 29
Psalm 63:6 16
Psalm 73:24 59
Psalm 77:12-14 23
Psalm 85:8 40
Psalm 88:13 18, 27

Dick B.'s Historical Titles on Early A.A.'s Spiritual Roots and Successes

Dr. Bob's Library: Books for Twelve Step Growth   (Second Edition)
Foreword by Ernest Kurtz, Ph.D., Author, *Not-God: A History of Alcoholics Anonymous*.
A study of the immense spiritual reading of the Bible, Christian literature, and Oxford Group books done and recommended by A.A. co-founder, Dr. Robert H. Smith. Paradise Research Publications, Inc.; 104 pp.; 8 1/2 x 11; velo bound; 1996; $15.50; ISBN 1-885803-11-7.

Anne Smith's Journal, 1933-1939: A.A.'s Principles of Success   (Second Edition)
Foreword by Robert R. Smith, son of Dr. Bob & Anne Smith; co-author, *Children of the Healer*.
Dr. Bob's wife, Anne, kept a journal in the 1930's from which she shared with early AAs and their families ideas from the Bible and the Oxford Group which impacted on A.A. Paradise Research Publications, Inc.; 192 pp.; 6 x 9; perfect bound; 1994; $15.50; ISBN 1-885803-01-X.

The Oxford Group & Alcoholics Anonymous: A Design for Living That Works (Second Edition)
Foreword by Rev. T. Willard Hunter; author, columnist, Oxford Group activist.
A comprehensive history of the origins, principles, practices, and contributions to A.A. of "A First Century Christian Fellowship" (also known as the Oxford Group) of which A.A. was an integral part in the developmental period between 1931 and 1939. Paradise Research Publications, Inc.; 432 pp.; 6 x 9; perfect bound; 1998; $17.95; ISBN 1-885803-19-2. (Previous title: *Design for Living*).

The Akron Genesis of Alcoholics Anonymous   (Newton Edition)
Foreword by former U.S. Congressman John F. Seiberling of Akron, Ohio.
The story of A.A.'s birth at Dr. Bob's Home in Akron on June 10, 1935. Tells what early AAs did in their meetings, homes, and hospital visits; what they read; how their ideas developed from the Bible, Oxford Group, and Christian literature. Depicts roles of A.A. founders and their wives; Henrietta Seiberling; and T. Henry Williams. Paradise Research Pub.; 400 pp., 6 x 9; perfect bound; 1998; $17.95; ISBN 1-885803-17-6.

The Books Early AAs Read for Spiritual Growth   (Sixth Edition)
An exhaustive bibliography and brief summary of all the books known to have been read and recommended for spiritual growth by early AAs in Akron and on the East Coast. Paradise Research Publications, Inc.; 74 pp.; 8 1/2 x 11; velo bound; 1997; $15.50; ISBN 1-885803-18-4.

New Light on Alcoholism: The A.A. Legacy from Sam Shoemaker
Forewords by Nickie Shoemaker Haggart, daughter of Rev. Sam Shoemaker; and Mrs. W. Irving Harris.
A comprehensive history and analysis of the all-but-forgotten specific contributions to A.A. spiritual principles and practices by New York's famous Episcopal preacher, the Rev. Dr. Samuel M. Shoemaker, Jr.—dubbed by Bill W. a "co-founder" of A.A. and credited by Bill as the well-spring of A.A.'s spiritual recovery ideas. Good Book Publishing Company; 416 pp.; 6 x 9; perfect bound; 1994; $19.95; ISBN 1-881212-06-8.

The Good Book and The Big Book: A.A.'s Roots in the Bible   (Bridge Builders Ed.)
Foreword by Robert R. Smith, son of Dr. Bob & Anne Smith; co-author, *Children of the Healer*.
The author shows conclusively that A.A.'s program of recovery came primarily from the Bible. This is a history of A.A.'s biblical roots as they can be seen in A.A.'s Big Book, Twelve Steps, and Fellowship. Paradise Research Publications, Inc.; 264 pp.; 6 x 9; perfect bound; 1997; $17.95; ISBN 1-885803-16-8.

That Amazing Grace: The Role of Clarence and Grace S. in Alcoholics Anonymous
Foreword by Harold E. Hughes, former U.S. Senator from, and Governor of, Iowa.
Precise details of early A.A.'s spiritual practices—from the recollections of Grace S., widow of A.A. pioneer, Clarence S. Paradise Research Pub; 160 pp; 6 x 9; perfect bound; 1996; $16.95; ISBN 1-885803-06-0.

Good Morning!: Quiet Time, Morning Watch, Meditation, and Early A.A.
A practical guide to Quiet Time—considered a "must" in early A.A. Discusses biblical roots, history, helpful books, and how to. Paradise Research Pub; 154 pp.; 6 x 9; perfect bound; 1998; $15.50; ISBN: 1-885803-09-5.

Turning Point: A History of Early A.A.'s Spiritual Roots and Successes
Foreword by Paul Wood, Ph.D., President, National Council on Alcoholism and Drug Dependence.
Turning Point is a comprehensive history of early A.A.'s spiritual roots and successes. It is the culmination of six years of research, traveling, and interviews. Dick B.'s latest title shows specifically what the Twelve Step pioneers borrowed from: (1) The Bible; (2) Rev. Sam Shoemaker's teachings; (3) The Oxford Group; (4) Anne Smith's Journal; and (5) meditation periodicals and books, such as *The Upper Room*. Paradise Research Publications, Inc.; 776 pp.; 6 x 9; perfect bound; 1997; $29.95; ISBN: 1-885803-07-9.

How to Order Dick B.'s Historical Titles on Early A.A.

Order Form

Qty.

Send:

__ *Turning Point* (a comprehensive history)	@ $29.95 ea.	$____
__ *New Light on Alcoholism* (Sam Shoemaker)	@ $19.95 ea.	$____
__ *The Oxford Group & Alcoholics Anonymous*	@ $17.95 ea.	$____
__ *The Good Book and The Big Book* (Bible roots)	@ $17.95 ea.	$____
__ *The Akron Genesis of Alcoholics Anonymous*	@ $17.95 ea.	$____
__ *That Amazing Grace* (Clarence and Grace S.)	@ $16.95 ea.	$____
__ *Good Morning!* (Quiet Time, etc.)	@ $15.50 ea.	$____
__ *Anne Smith's Journal, 1933-1939*	@ $15.50 ea.	$____
__ *Dr. Bob's Library*	@ $15.50 ea.	$____
__ *Books Early AAs Read for Spiritual Growth*	@ $15.50 ea.	$____

Shipping and Handling   Shipping and Handling** $____

Add 10% of retail price (minimum $3.75). ** Within U.S. only.
Special arrangements required for shipments outside the U.S.

Total Enclosed $____

Name: _____ (as it appears on your credit card)

Address: _____

City: _____ State: ___ Zip: _____

Credit Card #: _____ (MC VISA AMEX) **Exp.** _____

Tel. #: _____ Signature _____

Special Value for You!

If purchased separately, the author's ten titles would normally sell for $182.70, plus Shipping and Handling. Using this Order Form, you may purchase sets of all ten titles for **only $149.95 per set**, plus Shipping and Handling. Please contact us for Shipping and Handling charges for orders being shipped outside of the United States.

Please mail this Order Form, along with your check or money order, to: Dick B., c/o Good Book Publishing Company, Box 837, Kihei, HI 96753-0837. Please make your check or money order payable to "**Dick B.**" in U.S. dollars drawn on a U.S. bank. If you have any questions, please phone or fax: 1-808-874-4876. Dick B.'s email address is: dickb@dickb.com. The "**Dick B. [Internet] Home Page on Early A.A. history**": "http://www.dickb.com".